D0031431

Other Books by
KAREN ELIZABETH GORDON

THE TRANSITIVE VAMPIRE

THE WELL-TEMPERED SENTENCE

To Tom —

Intimate Apparel

Come into this
boudoir +
unlock
your mind — unbutton the alphabet
Best wishes,

Karen E. Gordon

Intimate Apparel

A DICTIONARY OF THE SENSES

Karen Elizabeth Gordon

TimesBOOKS

Brief portions of this work were previously published in *Exquisite Corpse* in 1983.

Library of Congress Cataloging-in-Publication Data

Gordon, Karen Elizabeth.
    Intimate apparel.

    1. English language—Context—Popular works.
I. Title.
PE1574.G67   1989   420'.207   88-40161
ISBN 0-8129-1222-5

Production Editor: Beth Pearson

Text design and illustrations by Marie-Hélène
Fredericks

Manufactured in the United States of America
9 8 7 6 5 4 3 2
First Edition

Full House

Closet Drama

Introduction

Ah, nothing in this world we live and dream is only what it seems. Here you have a dictionary that is *really* a storybook without a proper ending—just a provocatively improper one. The stories in this unrectilinear volume do not so much break off as they become attached to one another, while you form attachments to them, and to the characters whose stories they are: the hapless hypochondriac with his faulty kneecap and bar of anodyne soap; Bedruthan with *his* knees knocking in fear at the ocean's frothy edge, and the deadpan, deadly sensuous mermaid he seeks, to return a lost tortoiseshell comb; Yolanta expatriating on the Continent with her *langue maternelle*, her passport—and a bookmark between her legs; a sassy Cinderella, lost in reveries, breaking glasses in the dishwater, and unmasking social form and ceremony in her unabashed dealings with the prince; and many, many others, weaving in and out of each other while the two seamstresses, Elsbeth of the North and Anja of the South, stitch together their tattered tales and scattered lives into a fabrication they can *all* wear at once upon a time. And so can you. Baffled, perhaps, at first, you will find that you are slipping, slowly but silkily, into something more comfortable the further you read, the more familiar you become. Because this is an affectionate book that wants to be held, like any woman within it, and will hold your attention and call it back again to fulfill this most natural desire.

Fabric, fabrication—such is the stuff of these lost chronicles come together here. Swinging their hatboxes, swaying their hips, chapters with torn slips wander in on high heels and blistered feet. A wedding dress is being cut out and sewn by the same two seamstresses who are handstitching all these pieces into place, with time and meaning layered like the ultimate wedding cake.* A cloth of many colors unravels, interwoven as it is of the simply real, the fabulously real, and the purely imaginary, and the threads, of various lengths and glistenings—well, some are invisible, so a nearsighted *couturière* bent over them has declared. A cloth of ecstatic flannel, narrative handkerchief, and wrinkled linen moods; fur hands, satin of solitude, handled-with-carelessness glass shoes. Out of a tailor's dummy's muslin epidermis is the flesh made word.

Words themselves are the intimate attire of thoughts and feelings. Here they are turned inside-out to see what's going on beneath the surface of everyday presences, garments, and forms. And if a book can wear a jacket, the notion of a book can be turned inside-out, too—for much of the *story* here is in the notes, and not in the body of the text . . . the very body we find on the final undulation: nude with sunbeam for zipper. Facing things in this manner, we watch estrangements disappear. Death, whose name we avoid pronouncing, is just the girl next door.

Like a diaphanous nightgown, language both hides and reveals. There is no way of getting at the naked truth, even if it's wearing the Emperor's New Clothes, or the Empress's New Clothos. We follow our Mother Tongue into her boudoir, anyway, hoping for a glimpse of something never yet beheld—and come face to face with our own reflections in her most private mirror, veiled meanings in a gossamer heap on the floor. And still there are enough words left in the old girl's voice to sing us to sleep once again. "I've got *you* uncovered," she says.

* There are lots of cakes, being created and consumed, and cookie crumbs on the sheets of the alphabed. In *The Gingerbread Variations*, the cake itself is a consumer of lost little souls, the sweet tooth of childhood zigzagging them through the woods.

· A · B · C · D · E · F ·

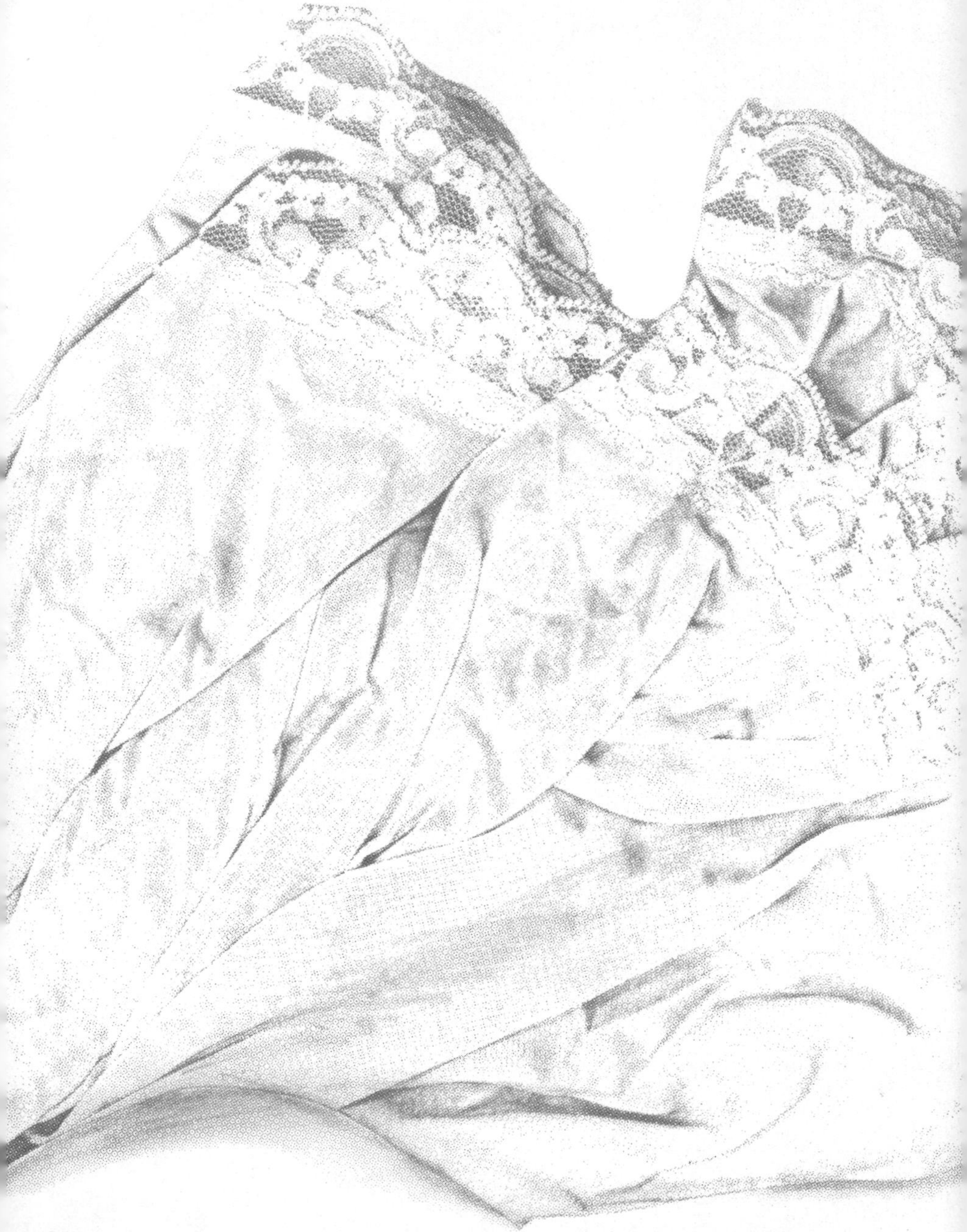

M · N · O · P · Q · R · S

Full House

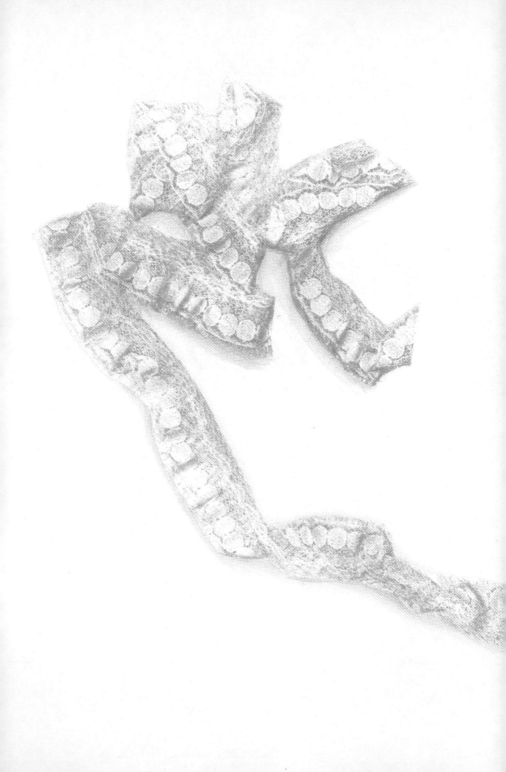

Absinthe

She drenched him with an absinthe regard.

A B S I N T H E

See DUSK; LIPS.

Well, you don't have to. I'll tell you right now that she proceeded to let out a wild shrill hiccup, and when he kept questioning her about the parchment enwrapping her salmon, and the lost Albanian, she excused herself to the powder room "and galloped off in a chorus of evasive whispers."

But you'll find yourself in their company again soon enough, wondering if dessert will *ever* arrive so he can lean across the table to ask, "Don't you want the rest of your clafouti?" and rend its remains with his fork.

Act

It was a meaningless act, but we knew its implications.

A C T

"a meaningless act"

One of the propositions subjected to philosophic inquiry in *Carnal Knowledge*. "The closeness that comes in handfuls" eludes one's grasp when "the metaphysical stuff gets out of hand."

Beast

(from *Life in the Forest Sauvage*)

> Down the alley slouched a beast
> en route to the Apocalypse.

B E A S T

Not all that rough a beast, this one. He had shaved that morning, and his swagging carriage made alluring ripples in the silk T-shirt on his back.

Books

The beautiful bones of Notre Dame crouch and soar in the light flooding stone and I shove myself through the door of Shakespeare and Company to read about Madame de Pompadour's love potions and the many-colored solitudes of Emily Dickinson. A swarthy English-speaking type approaches me, in unctuous wonder first at where we've met before, then why I could possibly like to read, arriving at his own inspired conclusion that "it must be something psychological," with which I can only agree. I ensconce myself in a chair but am soon to be lifted out of this attitude by an invitation to the library above. "I must lie down where all the ladders start in the foul rag and bone shop of the heart" points the way up a rough red stairway which is to be crawled, not walked, into a dimly lit affable claustrophobia of old books, ghosts, and somnambulists, big chairs in corners of sunken, slumbering structure, and a bed against one wall, covered in blue velvet and summoning up all the bibliophiles who must have sated their lusts in this room. I lean back and gratify some of my own, in a rapid succession of imaginary lovers who dematerialize after having their way with me and stealing a few books.

BOOKS

From Yolanta's PARIS column for *Exquisite Corpse*, that first "crossed legs in closed winter" year of exile and uncertainty, adventure and thwarted love. Expatriate translator, writer, and drifter, and Jacob's* Neoplatonic other, Yolanta is the eventual author of these motley collected works:

The Scarlet Slippers
The Read Letter
Maps and Tatters
Life in the Forest Sauvage: A Girlhood in Cosmopolis
A Crusty Baguette, a Cup of Beaujolais
You Darling Manflower: A Bestiary
Crossed Legs and Closet Winters

* Jacob Other: a would-be Renaissance man, but for his lumbosacral strain. Three times resisted Yolanta's entreaties that he consult the physician in Baden-Baden so highly recommended by other afflicted characters in this book.

Boudoir

He followed her into the delphiniums and irises of her private wallpaper and began speaking to her back and her three reflections, all wearing a pout—or a scowl— or was she biting her lip?

BOUDOIR

See the MUG of reconciliation.

Bread

A couple of *pains de campagne* (*pas trop cuits*) on her feet, and wrapped in a semblance of sanity she had donned for her matutinal tour of the *quartier*, Yolanta entered the *boulangerie* on the corner and requested a copy of *Manon Lescaut*.

B R E A D

Jacob Other, visiting Yolanta one afternoon in her *chambre de bonne*, found her popping two battered books into the toaster when he arrived for tea. The incident turned up in his essay (brief, as usual) "Déconfitures et tartines," which ended, perhaps because of the marmalade on her nightstand, "It all remains to be seen through; she is so good at guesswork she'll never put clothes on or find a literal meaning on the other side of the bed."

It was someone else, anyway, eating a toasted page in LIPS.

Bubbles

(from *The Glass Shoe*)

Dear father,

How you ever came to lay your head among the bosoms of this family is beyond my widest comprehension. I am trying, but my thoughts buckle back each time to the more essential question: how could you leave me here? I am writing to you at the end of my staggering day's work (yes, I sometimes stagger from exhaustion and hunger, for they feed me but poorly, and leave few crumbs on the white lacquer breakfast trays for me to scrape up on the way to the dishwater and the window that meets my gaze above the hot bubbles in the morning sun—such lovely rainbows on those swelling edges before they pop!). How often I have to remind myself that "This, too, shall pass," your words, and all that remains to fill the emptiness where once you were, with your dark and bracing odor and evening armchair repose like an animal after feeding at dusk.

After you left, they dropped all pretense of treating me as one of them, an accord I did not entirely rejoice in, anyway, as you will remember—you saw those sullen looks of accusation I would cast in your direction as I rolled little balls of bread along the edges of my plate and strained the dancing bubbles of mineral water through my teeth—and turned me into their fuliginous servant girl in overalls, with reddened knuckles and cracked heels. Before the others are stirring, I must be up and get the fire going, put out the milk bottles, and then I'm ladling the soured milk into bowls; baking brioche; grinding the coffee; tossing more wood onto the fire (wood I drag back from long rambles in the forest, in a cart that I pull like a frail young ox, swaying my head from side to side with my feet pointed outward to help keep my balance and keep from overturning the little logs already neatly stacked and crackling in the late summer sun); heating the day's first kettle of water over the merry flames for the coffee and all three sponge-baths I slather over each one as she lumbers out of sleep. I know that this ritual gives them the most satisfaction, allowing them to observe my humiliation up close—and then afterward there are the massages, as if I hadn't had enough with kneading the brioche and then the ba-guettes before tucking them under my own comforter to rise in the recent memory of my own sleepy warmth.

I spend my days slaving over their bodies, jumping every time one of them yells, "Hey, Ashtray!" scrubbing the house and polishing the mirrors and silver, preparing these luscious snacks, and living for those moments to myself when I am off on an errand in the village or am left alone while the three of them are out paying a call. You know that my disposition has always been bright, no matter what adversity comes along to tarnish my twinkle, that I always find some small pleasure to cup in my hands. And so I gnaw at the bones of my misfortune and count my *blessures* in the evanescent gleams of copper, soap, and glass. Father, dear, I am very tired, and must close up for the night. In my dreams, your hand holds the meaning of all this suffering, which I know cannot outlast my beauty and my youth.

B U B B L E S

"Hey, Ashtray!"
Some of their other nicknames for her were Dustrag, Mopsy, and Smudge. In one of her bubbly lamentations, Cinderella sighs, "I am a soap bottle in a flowered dress." So you see, she didn't *always* wear overalls. See SCHMATTE.

"And so I gnaw at the bones of my misfortune"
In *The Little Match Girl*, it's:

> "I was so hungry I started gnawing at my cuticles."

Cake

Eat your cake and make it too.

C A K E

"Eat your cake"

An entry in the diary as the big night approached suggests that Cinderella intended to do so:

"It's almost time to go to the ball, to get all glittered up (that'll pop their eyes out!) and hot under the arms, to sweat on the prince against his buttoned-up front while his hand slides down the back of my gown. Oh prince oh baby jump on me! Take me home to my *belle-mère* and my castle in the air,[1] and you'll sleep in my hair that even now unwinds to turn back time and polish the years in the suds the ashes and tears.[2] Your face on my belly, we'll calm down and discuss our wedding cake and how to frost it and how to cut our guests. How many little princes shall we beget and throw upon the land to slide down the banisters of our multi-layered *gâteau de noce* with its moat of many colors running red with blood and blue, while I go barefoot, no more defective clothing on my body, and sleep, oh yes, till noon.

[1] The author of *Reflections on a Slivered Shoe* must have been thinking of this passage when he wrote, "She stuck her foot in the firmament."

[2] Another diary entry: "Had a good long sob today. Well, not so much that I had to put out my little sign that says WET FLOOR."

Cake

(from *The Gingerbread Variations*)

She had a handsome profile and lived in a *gâteau* of her own making that she redecorated once a year, reinforcing the sagging sidings of gingerbread, spackling fissures with a vanilla glaze, and refrosting the entire façade with a design she would work out in the fall and winter months after planting the bulbs.

Candy

Don't get me started on Alfred again.
He showed up here the other night with
little paper bags over his ears.
How come? I says.
Want some penny candy, he says,
Your red-hot cinnamon heart.

C A N D Y

"paper bags"
In "The Introverted Attitude of the Intuitive-Feeling Type," a study of creativity by Jacob Other, we find: "He beats her and kicks her and she smiles on, clutching messages in paper bags." It's actually about someone enjoying a good night's sleep.

Circle

They were running viscous circles around each other in the depths of the treacle well.

Cloud

In the years, though, leading up to his demise—and you will remember that this was of his own free will, even if you don't agree that one has the right to take one's own life in the belief that that might make one feel better—

the hypochondriac derived joy from small miracles, and never looked for the black clouds over the silver linings that would suddenly appear in his skies. One such fine day, his aberrant kneecap was not troubling him much, so he skipped to the loo.

C L O U D

"aberrant kneecap"
For those readers who missed his pages in *The Transitive Vampire*—wearing shifting tenses, and a stoppered bottle— or those on whom the synopsis of his full tragedy left no lasting impression, it is repeated here:

> This story recounts the adventures of a hypochondriac who has been plagued by an aberrant kneecap and had tried several miracle cures and then takes matters into his own hands and drowned himself.

While we're at it: Timofey, the sempiternal lexicographer, appears in the early pages, and elsewhere in that same book— as the quaking hero of two other literary works.

Coffee

The waitress frisked her between her coffee and her raised eyebrows.

C O F F E E

See the first, the lonely TABLE.

Coffee

Alexander Pope, who had a constant headache during
the long disease his life, used to sniff coffee all day long
and nights in public houses to relieve the pulsing pain.
Like alcohol, coffee is a social drink: people are always
asking, "Do you want a cup of coffee?" when they mean,
"I wanna drag you to my bed." Coffee is also a necessary
ritual between the sheets and the streets. Bach wrote a
piece called "The Coffee Cantata" whose raucous laughter and jollity we can only attribute to the magic of the
drug. It's about a father who won't let his daughter marry
unless she gives up drinking coffee, but she outsmarts
the old man and has coffee written into the marriage
articles, and becomes the first bride in history to live
happily ever after.

C O F F E E

Galloping ahead to Istanbul before *Frangipani's Pajamas*, this
footnote is wondering if Bach was aware of the Ottoman
marriage laws, and how graciously and seriously they granted
a wife a lifetime of coffee in exchange for her total submission.

Comb

Bedruthan stepped lightly into the creamy waves clab-
bering the black rocks of the Cornish coast. His huge
body was unbalanced by this even more enormous,
oceanic motion and by the disorienting configuration of
cliffs fringed with gentle green grass that twinkled in
the early morning light like Elfina's eyes, and gorse that
prickled his calves and ankles when he exposed them to
the sweet climes of May. *This* was a peculiar sensation,
though: terrified of the water, never before had he dared
come this far into the foam crashing around his knees,
which knocked together while his teeth met in desperate

intervals. What mattered now, however, even more than his old trepidation, was that he find the mermaid whose comb* had washed up on the coarse sand.

* Had it paused in tidepools, to comb the fingers of sea anemones and tease the gelatinous amethyst defenses beneath that enticing act? Scraped the backs of starfish along spiny radii from point to center to point? The comb, made of real tortoiseshell, just like the tortoise Arthur Gordon Pym had eaten, was so tiny in his big rough hands.*

* Bedruthan had problems with dry skin and chapping. When he was a child, his father had smeared his hands with lamb fat (collected from the drippings caught in the preparation of the evening meal) and then covered this mess with socks. (Funny, these, too, came from sheep, the very ones who grazed a bit farther inland, in Devon, but since these giants' legs reached into the very skies where the vigorous little depressions come from that are responsible for the vicissitudes of the English weather, it took no time at all to skip over there and return with a lamb or two kicking and bleating beneath the provider's armpit.) And these socks he stuck Bedruthan's chafed paws in as he tucked the little giant into his bed.*

* Little Bedruthan slept in a bed modeled after the Viking ones you can see to this day in the open-air museum outside Oslo and while you're at it ponder the origins of the pillow, that handy prop on the connubial couch. The Vikings slept in beds that rose up at an angle, lifting the torso of one or another of these pillaging brutes* higher than his lower half.

* Well, they weren't all brutes; most, in fact, were peaceful settlers seeking new breezes in which to set up house. But the brutes—did they, too, sometimes stray through the salted waters with lost baubles and bottles of eau de toilette looking for the nereids from whose nacreous grasp these objects had slipped? Did they ever feel anything like tenderness before the drenched beauty of these pelagic girlbeasts whose skin was kept atomized and

luminous by spray just like the modern French mannequin's face fogged with Evian? And did these creatures grab their combs when they saw the prows bobbing up and down, and start sorting the algae and bracken out of their hair and rubbing the barnacles off the napes of their necks? Bedruthan wondered this and many other things to disport his attention far from his faltering steps.

C O M B

"find the mermaid"
Deep blue cheesecake. A girl with long hair waving about in the water and very scaly skin below the waist, despite hours spent in her grotty boudoir trying to make it sleek. Knocking about the Seven Seas and more, adrift in the Gulf Stream off England. In *Frangipani's Pajamas*, back to the Bosporus!

"nacreous"
From the same mother as Pearl.

"fogged with Evian"
Mise en bouteille au ruisseau.

Come

Come to my senses and get into my drift.

C O M E

One of the songs of the mermaids in COMB. Also given to beckoning with invitations like, "Come on over and handle my submerged company." But don't imagine it was always easy, singing the sailors to their deaths. Mermaids were known at times to wipe tears from the drowning men's eyes with their own hair, and dash at their own cheeks furtively with handkerchiefs pulled out of their victims' pockets. You could find these handkerchiefs stashed beneath rocks on the ocean floor as tender mementos of secret regrets and big wet salty kisses exchanged before the bloating set in.

Couch

Oh, I love talking with him! He puts all
these couches to lie down on in his sentences.

C O U C H

Yolanta gushing over Jacob's crushing velvet voice and cushy syntax—although on the rare occasion when he'd drag her to a literary soirée, she often lost him in the crowd. Wending her way among the *"c'est évident, non?"*s and the *"n'est-ce pas,"*s of frank intercourse, she'd wind up in a corner stuffing words in edgewise, batting them against the walls, and making thumbnail sketches of the citizens inhabiting this crumbling *gâteau*.

Cup

Morpheus, in the bottom of this cup of drowsiness, I can see another cup. I knew I was dying of thirst. It's all there, encircled, embraced, how those hours held us and gave us to one another, the room disappearing around us from the moment you came in. I needed to lie still and sleepless beside you, and those final touches, to see you there on that side of the day and in the wide edges between waking and sleep, your hand moving over me, pushing the pillows more closely around me, giving me this extra voluminous body on the sheets almost creamy against my chafed, still stinging skin. I wanted to cry, "Don't leave me! I'll report you for desertion—for abandoning a woman in bed!" as the door opened to the vast terrible daylight swallowing you right out of my arms, and throwing your shadow halfway round the earth. Another time, my love, a hotel with room service, or maybe some snowbound cabin, our frostbitten fingers, extending gracefully from their lustrous knuckles, caressing each other over a salver of Smyrna figs.

C U P

"a salver of Smyrna figs"
From Izmir and the land of *Frangipani's Pajamas*, as that traveling shadow attests. Further reading on this shameless fruit in Alexandre Dumas's *Dictionnaire de cuisine. Ecco il fico!*

Dark

(from *The Gingerbread Variations*)

Our flesh crept about the room as we
huddled there together in the dark.

D A R K

Gretl, recounting the ghastly incarceration in that delectable,
fragrant house—amidst the flashbulbs and brouhaha that
greeted the children's return to their father's shack. She said
a lot of stuff that wasn't true, as long as she had them there
eating up her every word:

> "... the ground opened up at these words and we found
> ourselves in a dripping cavern with all sorts of gewgaws
> hanging out of its cracks. But what came after this is so
> dreadful that it would distress me to say any more ..."

Dollar

Stretch your dollar over my body.

D O L L A R

Yolanta to some guy, fellow American, in line at the Bureau
de Change. Two weeks later found her painting the *salon* and
salle d'entrée for a French colonel in Boulogne instead, and
taking tremendous liberties with the classics in his *bibliothèque*. We can surmise the monologue she delivered to her
compatriot—from the last work in which she figured as a
dubious, cameo character:

> Yolanta seemed to think that everyone in the world had
> read "Rameau's Nephew Meets Rappacini's Daughter";
> she referred to it in every conversation she had. This
> was only one of the signs of her coming dementia (many

more were yet to manifest themselves); her delusions became progressively more literary and bizarre.

Door

Her door ajar, she came unhinged.

D O O R

"Her door ajar"
I don't know what was lurking in the corridor and about to jump her, but the phrase brings to mind both JAR and the terrors of Timofey, making his comeback in MIRROR. "I left the marble ajar" is how he would put it to himself on his fearful forays after dusk (*"dans les ténèbres,"* the French translation reads), thinking fondly of his nice slab (it was even starting to grow a little moss!) in the cemetery and the smell of resin still clinging to his wooden box, and wishing (for this one night!) he could just stay at home.

Door

"You're distressing my innocence," protested the in-genue of the twinkling breasts and feline haunches as she got past the door of waiting and into the room of womanhood.

D O O R

"You're distressing"
After Henry Purcell's "Distressed Innocence Suite." An ear-lier aversion begins: "You're distressing my innocence, sweetie." But she was maybe not so sweet or innocent; a later episode in the suite, anyway, says:

He pursued her gentle refusal to have a good time with him through an endless corridor of locked doors and pleasant alcoves hung with rubbings of her earlier amours.

Door

. . . then there was this whispery sound, like an envelope sliding under a door and over a carpet . . .

(Note to artist: Paint a pattern of Oriental carpet that is also somehow the contents of the envelope.)

D O O R

"Oriental carpet"
The carpet flew back to its homeland before I could read the letter and tell you what it said.

Door

The molting flamingos crowded around the doorway in gaping attitudes of incredulity as Torquil and Jonquil staggered out for a postprandial snack two hundred fifty hours into their acquaintance, which they were eager to further debauch.

D O O R

With only four hours to get through, if this is the same place we last met them, in another book:

Their rendezvous at the Last Judgment Pinball Machine Motel turned into a 254-hour marathon that neither Torquil nor Jonquil would ever regret.

Door

Then there was this rapping at the door and many glasses clattered to the table at once and someone declaimed in broken accents that surely it must be an uninvited guest come to slaver amongst them and not a messenger of dire tidings to ruin their revels just yet.

D O O R

See the TABLE of unfinished childhoods.

Door

Death, that pickled strumpet, is
just the girl next door.

D O O R

"girl next door"
Jacob Other in *Eros and Thanatos* traces her development from a gawky child into a vamp* you'd give your false teeth for a night with: her pigtails, stuffed animals, and tricycle; the Girl Scout cookies and braces; the AA-cup bra and first strapless gown, nights out in back seats of cars.

* In *Frangipani's Pajamas*, we find her as one of the girls in the seraglio with her own tales to tell, of fatal embraces and desperate cries. Her kinship with the mermaids is also under scrutiny.

Drawers

(from *The Glass Shoe*)

No lust lost between me! They were out quaffing Dar-
jeeling and squashing their bustles on overstuffed chairs,
so I dropped my dustcloth, sluffed off my rags, and
prowled the *boudoirs* and *salles de bain* to my heart's
content, breaking into jars of colors and powders, twirling in petticoats, and giving myself lingering looks in
an oval mirror, my amphitheater. I frizzed my bangs,
parted my glances, twined my tendrils around my temples, then dumped a few bottles of Veuve Clicquot into
a tub of hot water for a bubble bath. Still wet and effer-
vescing I glistened over pieces of furniture, hugging my
knees and trying to picture the prince in black pajamas
about to slide from his waist. But I didn't get far with
this vision, never having seen as much as his face, so I
got up and went riffling through drawers sniffing sachets,
silk, potpourris, flopped back on a mound of cushions,
and I put my finger in that little place where time
twitches and spent the rest of the afternoon quietly trea-
cling myself.

D R A W E R S

Concatenations on the letter *t*, starting with the unmentioned
teacups.

Dusk

In the crepitating dusk of clatters and whispers, he
traced each hollow in her candlelit complexion, taking
an occasional stab at some veiled meaning that clung to
her words as the sea roared on in his Coquilles St. Jacques.

Face

I toy with a cup of *café express* on the Place Gambetta,
a well-behaved *quartier*, for most of the people who live
here are dead. Apollinaire lies in nearby Père Lachaise.
Through one of those creepy sensataions that are forever
crawling over me, I become aware of the stranger at the
table next to mine and turn to stare openly at him. As
he obligingly or coquettishly turns away his face, I can
study his right cheek at my leisure: a poem carved by I
know not what sharp and eloquent sort of blade—Burma
Shave haiku? It looks like this, but Fenellosa is not avail-
able to tell me what it means:

A hearing aid is poised above this very interesting
wound, and as I believe it is listening to what I am thinking, I think I had better leave. On the 69 bus from Gambetta to St. Paul, Raymond Queneau's *Exercises in Style*
is played by all the passengers, for we all take turns
treading on each other's toes and uttering mild or serious
oaths. I am confronted on this bus with another ideogram
carved into the left cheek of an imperious and frowning
blonde. But even her frown is not of the moment; someone has left it there:

F A C E

"study his right cheek"

Running her eyes over whatever reading matter Paris held out to her, Yolanta throwing herself into her unrecompensed work as Paris correspondent for that rambunctious literary review.

Face

**They've been unmasked, and they're
trying to save what faces they have left.**

F A C E

"what faces they have left"

During the play within a play of MACARONI where all the Commedia del Arte regulars—Pantalone, Burattino, Grattiano, Pierrot, Arlecchino, and even Columbine in a suit and Nikes with pantyhose—are dressed up as bureaucrats in a modern totalitarian democratic state, several masks at once take turns sliding off one or another of the actors' faces, and the face-saving grimaces call for some pretty fast reflexes and snazzy pantomiming through the rapidly flickering changes on stage. It's a relief for everyone when the troupe shoves off at last for Pula, its colosseum, and another engagement, to which Anja had bought tickets weeks in advance for herself and a gorgeous brute, all six-foot-seven of him, from Montenegro, actually the sweetest fellow ever to pad through her house in a dressing gown, and whose incredible mustaches and revolver no longer caused her the least dismay.

Face

She greeted him with a sawed-off smile.
He brought her fragile face into focus
and shot her full of questions.

F A C E

"and shot her full of questions"
When Yolanta was hauled in to the Préfecture de Police by a pair of surly *gendarmes* for a little disturbance she had caused on the rue du Roi de Sicile, "they floodlighted her with questions,* and she blinked in helpless confusion, groping for the switch that would silence the roaring from that inimical circle of importunate mouths."

* Things did not get off to a good start with these fellows. She didn't even bother to answer their preliminary interrogations in French, replying to *"Votre prénom?"* with "Sweetie, I am Charles Bukowski trapped in the heart of Emily Dickinson," and so on.

Farewell

(from *Life in the Forest Sauvage*)

"Some enchanting evening this has been!" she exclaimed at her coy hostess, pocketing the rest of the handshake and seeing herself through the wrought irony gates of the woman's untoward farewell.

F A R E W E L L

"the rest of the handshake"
She'd been disagreeable ever since the *métro* station en route, where a *gamine de clocharde*, a bottle of *très très ordinaire* sloshing around in *her* ample pocket, had lifted the gloves right off her hands. See GLOVES.

Feather

Torquil, the pink feather that clung to my slipper as one eye opened to the morning and the shoes you were pulling on to walk you away from me: it really *was* pink; it wasn't the rosy fingers of dawn crawling over the carpet. So that claque of flamingos was there, their eyes loud with astonishment—or am I anthropomorphizing again?—and it wasn't being famished or delirious making me see things, their fluffy bodies and undulant necks, though I did wonder, afterward, when we returned from that sleazy coffee shop and they were gone.

Jonquil

Fever

(from *The Red Shoes*)

"And what have you been ingesting, little girl, to bring on these indecorous metamorphoses?"

Her feet glowed with shame. Oh, wretched radiance! The doctor wept in his patient's new fuchsia garden. Only the doctors took her body seriously! His amber bottles glittered on the floor-to-ceiling shelves, essences of stones, of herbs, of plagues. He grabbed the hem of her skirt to hold her still, sat her down, then stroked the arch inside one of the red shoes, before the needles and further questions, getting closer to the trouble, farther away from the pain. Her spine arched, her face curved away, then returned, her eyes steadied themselves in his as he took her out of them.

"This child is suffering from an early onset of depravity—an insouciance that so exceeds all possible hidden warmth that it gives her a feverish glow, a fever that flows in the dark."

F E V E R

On her way out of Herr Doktor's praxis and this initial consultation, she encountered a dashing man of handsome middle age limping into the waiting room humming a few bars from *Der Rosenkavalier*, which he'd seen in Vienna the week before. Their visits with this wizard put them both in high hopes and buoyant spirits: he bounced out later with a bar of soap in his hand headed for a double espresso at the Eis-Café Capri, and she could hardly wait to get back to the hotel and start stimulating her lymphatics! But first there had been some dark and difficult moments she would never forget, because while "insouciance" is what the doctor wrote in his notes to put in her file, what he said to her face was, "I like your *désinvolture*," a word with which she was unfamiliar, so it was easy to hear this as "the design of your vulture" and assume he was trying to tell her in an imagistic way that she had only a few weeks to live.

Floor

(from *The Glass Shoe*)

In the limpid depths and troubled waters of her eyes, he discerned portents of fiendish devotion, scrubbed floors and manicured gardens, and not a hint of the adulterous frivolity nibbling away at her soul. Oh, no, no one would ever be able to say of *her*, a tumbler of ice cubes melting in his hand as he turned to a friend and continued with his story, ". . . then this little mop of a woman came in scooting across the tiles . . ."

F L O O R

See sheet MUSIC, and Cinderella's coloring book its note will astound you with. Probably a wife-to-be keeping clear of the corners, à la *Don Juan Is a Woman* wearing SOCKS.

Fun

Are you a way to have fun, or
are you just another whack at
being?

F U N

She was the sort of girl who would waylay some man she'd never laid eyes on, happily bearing flowers to the girl he lived with, and beguile the bouquet right out of his hand, bending his homeward steps elsewhere—just for the fun of it!

Fur

And this, *this* is winter, this great skinned cat whose haunches ache and swell with the arthritic vapors curling out of the Seine, this cat whose whiskers tickle in the pause of thresholds, and whose consolations are bright and crackling, the ball of yarn to tangle with over its shuddering, furless frame.

F U R

"the ball of yarn to tangle with over its shuddering, furless frame"
Sounds more like the structure of this book than a description of winter, if you ask me.

Glass

. . . and so he poured all the most noble of
sentiments into an unfortunately shaped glass.

G L A S S

"into an unfortunately shaped glass"
From the chapter "Standing Water" in a curious work of
nineteenth-century decadence comparing love, in all its forms
(its "liquid frameworks") to this element. Jonquil had doubt-
lessly read the book shortly before writing her letter in RAIN.

Gold

Nibbling on an occasional wild berry or the golden meat
of a chanterelle on the damp northern island, the emaciated author fashioned lyrical passages out of faraway
fragrances while the impostor trampled little lettuces
and baby squash blossoms in the fertile soil of her distant
empire of a sham Provence.

G O L D

I'm sorry, but I don't know what this fraudulent-identity non-
sense is all about. Why would anyone want to impostor an
author? Unless the two of them had some sort of arrangement
so that the pale (BODICE) emaciated author could bang away
on her misty island in peace. But why was she pale? The
impostor part of this sundered duo is aglow in a radiant sun,
and the swollen bodice also makes her an unlikely fill-in for
the writer's gaunt bearing, hunched shoulders, and lackluster
indifference to food. Apart from these two fragments, there's
nothing more about them: nothing pastoral about the prose
anywhere else that I can see, and as for the lyricism, well,
see Céline in the notes to the Byzantine T-shirt (Hmm. Yeats,

too, lived on a damp northern island, with some far-fetched theory about multiple selves, something the hypochondriac was looking into when he got involved with the Theosophists in London). Is the conjugal bed at the same latitude as the chanterelles? There are no botanical flourishes to the author's side of the story in BODICE, so maybe she went to the island alone?

Hand

(from *Life in the Forest Sauvage*)

He held out his hand, but she didn't offer hers, and so it was an empty gesture.

H A N D

"but she didn't offer hers"
Introduction at that dinner party of the same moody guest taking her leave in FAREWELL.

Hand

In "The Glass Arachnid," nature enters on eight precise yet broken legs, tracking blood across the page, and it's only after you've turned to the next one that you realize it's not art that bleeds, but your own utilitarian and mutilated hand.

H A N D

"The Glass Arachnid"
A review by Jacob Other, a critic of contemporary poetry and prose, and himself the author of two books of poetry, *Winged Sheets* and *The Wronged Number*, both from Echolalia Press. "Wrestling with ideas is my favorite sport," says Jacob, who has a bad back. Hansel and Gretl's witch also had trouble with her back, wrenched in one of her battles against the elements munching away at her form-and-function house. She would soak in the tub, mumbling incantations, and then put ginger compresses over the snarled muscles as she lay on her belly before the hearth upon a rug of—no, I can't tell you what.

Handkerchief

Morpheus, off hoochy-koochying in someone else's bedroom, apparently, had stood her up three nights in a row.

When Morpheus finally did show up, as if nothing had happened, as if he hadn't left her alone night after night, to flatten her body out over the mattress like a starfish, digging her nails into its sides, she gave way to a tirade of bitter reproaches, jealous rantings, the tears of an abandoned child, and only after he took her into his arms and murmured her name and some smutty endearments did she fall into a heavy, exhausted slumber like a soaked and twisted handkerchief.

Hands

(from *The Gingerbread Variations*)

She was starved for company, and especially adored little visitors in short pants and wool jumpers stumbling through her neck of the woods in a famished condition and holding consanguine hands.

Hands

(from *The Little Match Girl*)

I struggled out with my *allumettes* and blew through the snow from door to door dressed in my fur cap and hands. I ought to explain about the hands. They were stitched together and wrapped about my throat and tossed over my left shoulder with some fingers pointing down my back. I could not afford a professional manicure, but the nails, well kept, and polished with Alabastro, gleamed in the moonlight thrown at them from the dazzling swath I cut in my reindeer boots.

It was Noel, and I passed many windows stuffed with patresfamilias displaying their generous sides before fireplaces in which silver paper occasionally flared, or a green ribbon, over logs from our northern forests, of pine, of spruce, of fir. My nostrils flared in forgetful pleasure as I passed through zones of various smokes blending in ever different combinations, and here and there paused to sniff deeply of them.

Then I came to a large window that returned me to my other senses, and I remembered as I looked through it at the swollen movements of grandmothers being indulgent and the smug contentment of three generations all feasting at once about the cold piercing my bones and my wretched blanket in a corner at home where we were lucky to burn coal if there were anything to burn, let alone eat, at all, and how I couldn't even go back there for shelter if not warmth without selling the matches. My own hands were cold because they were bare and wrapped around my tray of matches in such a way that I couldn't dig them into my cuffs and keep a grip on the merchandise. I may sound rather blasé about this now, but I was growing more bitter and frozen at each step which returned me always to this same window no matter which direction I attempted to follow, and I had to keep cajoling myself out of the snowdrifts of self-pity I kept sliding into, which is easy when there's no one to talk to, and you're half-crazed from hunger and not quite numb enough for oblivion. Had one door that night been opened to me in the most tentative of gestures, I would not have hesitated just because I looked a fright and my manners were only half polished from what I'd learned by watching through windows of other houses like this one on spring evenings in drawing rooms. Christmas forgives all shortcomings, accepts the chipped tooth, the little asymmetries that make each of us who we are, perfect in the very arrangement of aberrations by which we embody the hope and teleology of the human form.

"the dazzling swath I cut in my reindeer boots"
Someone else was responsible for her wardrobe in Renoir's
La Petite Marchande aux Allumettes. An officer on his way to
his wassails pauses to size up the situation and her feet, saying,
"With shoes like those you'd be better off at home."

A more ardent lover come to court *la petite** arrives on
a deserted stage set shortly thereafter to announce: "I have
an appointment with Karen tonight. I am DEATH!"

* Nowhere in this film does he or anyone else break into song with:

> *Allumetta, gentille Allumetta,*
> *Allumetta, je te fumerai.*
> *Je te brûlerai les fesses,*
> *Je te brûlerai les fesses.*
> *Allumette! Allumette! Oh!*

ℋoney

Morpheus, you came to me last night wearing earrings
and you bangled into bed with shiny skin like a dark
lady gleaming with secret siestas, a thousand and one
tricks up her stockings, and something else to be taken,
not given, and not for her to decide. I pulled you to me,
pawing your breasts that rose in my hands like bread
made of honey and the finest durum wheat, and you
moaned and rolled over so I could admire your back
shuddering each kiss I tasted of it, coming before you
could wonder what the world was coming to as it came
to meet you with each pulsing, answered plea. I wrapped
you in my nightgown, the one you tore once twisting
me out of it, just a slash along the hole my arm reached
out from to get at you, and held your head in my lap in
the turn it now was mine to sing you to sleep in this dark
night of our body reversed. My little girl, visions of sugar
daddies dancing in her head, my little paloma, my big

woman of a jukebox at rest. You arrived in a cloud of
smoke, damp and glowing, and the faces you showed me
kept waking me through the late mooning hours, so that
by dawn I was discursing on them, finally finding the
dream tongue to speak the cat had made off with into
the shadowed walls you brought down. My hand, soaked
in your colors, reached for you when I awoke at noon,
nothing but a strand of long black hair on the pillow to
tell me the truth. Later, in red shorts and shiny legs,
someone who seemed to have escaped one of those faces
to haunt my waking, smearing her lips and slicking down
her hair on the way to the elevator we shared. Darling,
I know you're out there, in bright daylight, beads of
moisture on your mother-of-pearly upper lip, your hips
so slightly swinging as you cast your eyes down shyly
and ask, "Breasts, where are you going?" and their silence
sounds the roundness off the dress I can't catch you in.

H O N E Y

Although obviously one of the *Sonnets to Morpheus*, which are
not sonnets at all, and are an insult to Rilke, as well as to his
many fine translators, viz. Stephen Mitchell and Edward
Snow, this piece seems to be also part of another work, *The
Troubled Succubus*.

"of the finest durum wheat"
More often found in pasta, but this is such a tangled mess of
mixed metaphor that it's not really so out of place.

Hotel

I fled headlong into the unknown man.
His navel is my hotel.

"His navel is my hotel"
Which must be the place, and not the frayed POCKETS of silken misery Yolanta is thinking of when she writes elsewhere in her notebooks: "I love my little hotel."

House

(from *The Gingerbread Variations*)

Aren't you wondering how she baked her gingerbread house? It's such a grotesque process that I don't want to frighten you with all the details, but I will tell you this much: she cooked it with her own body. And she could get quite mawkish about her own childhood while she was tampering with the oven's thermostat or shoving one of the youngsters through its see-through door.

Jar

He conducted a William Carlos Williams tour of her soul, fingering the implements in her kitchen cupboards, rattling her cake pans, imploring her jelly molds, pushing her around in her red wheelbarrow, and holding in a certain light her jar, which was not in Tennessee.

J A R

"in her red wheelbarrow"

Yolanta, during her "no ideas but in things" phase. The jar, which was empty, contained all her notions of "home." Sitting there on its American windowsill, it became the focus of Yolanta's nostalgia, and the object (recipient? receptacle?) of numerous yearning postcards over those years she spent abroad.

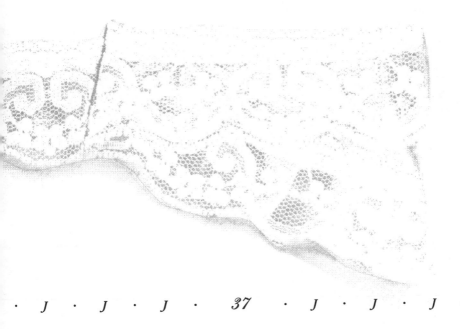

Kiss

What're you doing—cleansing my palate?

K I S S

See note to second LUNCH, not the one with crumbs of kulebyaka scattered over the table and leftover grechaniki and onions.

Lap

Torquil, I'd say I was surprised to hear from you, but I thought I passed you on the street the other day, so I figured you'd be showing up. We were in Paris, and we both skirted opposite edges of an open manhole. There was a unicorn at the bottom of it, waiting for a virgin to lay her head in its lap. But no virgin came (though they sometimes do), and this unicorn was battering its horn. No wonder we swayed across the street ensemble, darling, ensemble, between headlights, horizons, coffee, and dessert.

Jonquil

L A P

"between headlights, horizons, coffee, and dessert"

In those trysts with Torquil, coffee acted as an aphrodisiac for Jonquil, and thus acquired the mystique of rite and symbol in which her clamoring cup rejoiced. The drink appears in every allusion she makes to her lover, so that even the cooling of her passion for him is expressed in terms a Costa Rican economist would *con mucho gusto* comprehend:

> I awoke in the snow at the
> bottom of the coffeepot.

Leer

(from *The Glass Shoe*)

"And whose womb did you wamble out of, little girl?" leered a rheumatic marmaduke, breathing deeply on his lorgnette, polishing it off, and scrutinizing my porcelain cheeks.

"a rheumatic marmaduke"
Lorgnette and all restraint cast aside, a duke who had eaten
too freely of Yolanta's toast and marmalade before popping
up at the ball.

It took Cinderella a fortnight to record her many impressions,
panoramic and pointillist, of the ball—and that's *nothing* com-
pared to Anja's months of pawing through splintered portraits
and reportage to sort out which face belongs with which body,
let alone whom the ensemble was dancing or flirting with, or
trying to evade or pursue, and what was said to or thought
of whom, and at what critical moment the prince's big foot
came down with a terrible pressure and show-stopping tinkle
upon the handle-with-care glass shoe.

Legs

Effie and the catty little clique of nymphs she ran around
with would gather in the afternoon shadows of laurel
and cypress, giggling over their hot and panting pur-
suers, gobbling confections of rose water and walnuts,
and waxing each other's legs.

The faun, fagged out and disgusted after five years of
Effie's evasions among the Mediterranean flora, took up
with a Teuton named Hilda and departed for her home
in the Schwarzwald in a silver Mercedes Benz.

L E G S

"hot and panting"
Close in feeling is Yolanta's review in *Passion* of a poetry
reading she rated, as a pick-up joint, Hot to Trot:

> It was a good chance to mince about on bruised forelegs
> among ungulate brethren pricking forward ears of aug-

mented attention to the beckoning snorts of randy mares.

Light

She couldn't tell whether the paper she held in her hand was blue or green. She had to be absolutely sure. Green she could never send. There wasn't a single light in the house she could trust.

L I G H T

"Green she could never send"
See also the somnolent, refrigerated ponies in SALT. The color appears again in Yolanta's alliterative rendering of the backdrop in *The Toes of Nichevo*:*

Alone asking no greenness nor gardens   no
antelopes   no ancestors   Alone we dance

* Nichevo is the beer-drinking neuter pronoun tracking water into the footnote of TOWEL.

Lips

As she sawed into the parchment in which her *saumon aux roses fumées* had been baked, several random phrases (something about a tin goat and an Albanian losing his way) caught his incredulous eye across the table, but before he could raise his eyebrows to the level of astonishment he did in fact feel, she had lifted the toasted page to her lips and swallowed it, and all was lost once again.

Every sentence that fell from her lips was some sort of cliffhanger, or else a proverb in partita form—and now this! With her food!

The night was not yet embroidered with sequins. In fact, the evening has not worn on much further than where we left this couple in DUSK.

"an Albanian"
This evanescent and woebegone wanderer was a key figure in the attachment Anja (of FROCK) so precipitately formed for the tailor's dummy on the ship. Tatters of *The Secret of the Lost Albanian* kept popping up in the stories her Aunt Milanka had embroidered *her* childhood with—and here, years and life stories later, a chance encounter with an attractive speechless stranger at sea was delivering some of the original manuscript (long lost) into her own needleworking hands. Read SCAR very SOON. It was thus that Anja determined to bundle the dummy back to Istria—and became the mastermind of the book now held in *your* hands.

Lunch

About this week's meeting of the Slavic Gastronomes: You forgot to eat the caviar I forgot to offer you. You also missed Boris, in fine form and offering me "a piece of coffee," on a Russian poet who remains in a dark room in Minsk: "He has his cup of dirt in that life there."

Next week will be at Bougival, outside the gates of Turgenev's dacha and birch trees overlooking the Seine.

Menu (prix fixe): Vasko's Popovers, Alexander's Pushovers, Crimean Punishments, and Dead Soles
And some torrents of spring in a carafe
Yolantska
Pavelovna

L U N C H

"at Bougival"

After a slight detour into the unappetizing but brilliant story "The Rat Catcher," by Alexander Grinevski, or Grin, they went on to discuss narration in the later Russian writers, and clinked their glasses of vodka[1] in total agreement that the real masterpieces were written in either the first person peculiar or the third person deranged. This goes for chaps like Kuprin and Olesha as well as the better known dog[2] and madman of Gogol's little gem.

[1] Little realizing that in so doing they were coming perilously close to falling into the blini woman's borscht.

[2] "The style is very jerky. You can see that it's not written by a man. She starts off all right and then lapses into dogginess."
—*The Diary of a Madman*

Lunch

**She was so hungry for knowledge
she ate a professor for lunch.**

L U N C H

Probably the same graduate student* or avid scholar in this sequence from *Carnal Knowledge*, its pursuit after dark:

She spent the evening dodging the captious interjections of an educated imbecile bent on hauling her off to his bed in a riptide of her own sapience gone astray.

The minute he touched her she started lucubrating.

* If it *was* the graduate student, then at least the first of these is about her. The epigraph to her philosophy dissertation says:

If there's something more to know,
I don't want to.

Macaroni

COMMEDIA DEL ARTE SCENARIO

They have their antics.
They cavort about the plate of macaroni.
Quips and antics follow.
The magician weaves a few incantations and the
satyr is transformed into an emancipated woman.
He shambles into the grotto.
The nymph scrapes some lichen off the trees
and attempts to plaster it to her body.
They organize a holiday in Istria and set off
across the Adriatic with much further *adieux*.

Mad

She walked in and started battering him
with this HUGE VOICE.

M A D

"and started battering him"
From *The Battering Bride*, a ballet the girl in red shoes (and
oh, they felt heavy that night! especially during *Tulle Eulen-
spiegel's Merry Pranks*) attended while careening through Bo-
hemia to Gottwaldov, where the curator at the Museum of
Shoes awaited her with a covetousness quite overshadowing
the purely professional curiosity his letter had expressed.

Mirror

Timofey trembled. His terror was beginning once again.
Night was daubing at the twilight, closing in on the
world about him and crushing his spirits. No comfort at
all that he was a spirit himself! He scratched his head

with his ghost limb, knowing, and it was a dreadful knowledge, that he would soon have to go out into the street.

Nadia was polishing her nails. Her curtains were open, letting the soft night air in on her face, a chiaroscuro caress, considering the light bouncing off the glass. She felt something stirring in the air apart from that erotic crepuscular breath, a menace she could not put her finger on, a horror she could not name. She felt something rise within her, a longing, a cry, yet her body remained rigid, holding itself onto the moment as something toppled inside her and broke. At the same time she heard a soft crash like a fingernail falling through the branches of the tree outside her yawning curtains. She stiffened, closing her hand around the bottle on the table before which she sat. In the mirror, her face, and another face behind it, less opaque than hers. Both faces wore startled expressions of speechlessness with gaping mouths and sundered lips. He was back! Timofey! His hands were on her neck, lightly poised along the veins. His unmistakeable touch. Nadia's cleavage heaved quietly as in the days when there had been flesh on these fingers which were now of a creepy diaphanous substance, and smelling of subterranean depths.

Timofey *was* speechless. He was busy reading her thoughts. They read like a cheap tabloid and he was wishing he'd never come. His hands wandered farther down over her marble breasts. She was every bit as cold as he had been these last two years underground. This life had no more to offer him than the nebulous realm in which he had been ambling, bumping into other shades and having cozy little chats! he gathered, and he left the way he had come. He did not look back at her as he departed. And she had eyes only for herself.

A chapter from *Tidings of Timofey*, a Russian ghost story about a specter afraid of the dark. The literary chatter at the Slavic Gastronomes' LUNCH never sank to this level of tawdry entertainment.

"polishing her nails"
The color was Afterwards Verbena, one of a dozen bottles of Emily Dickinson nail lacquers she had recently purchased from a wandering minstrel and cosmetics salesman.* Nadia had just rubbed off some chipped and outgrown The Rose Is Out of Town, and had deliberated as the sun was setting among Interrogate the Daisies, Later the Peach, and Shrill Felicity before settling on this not too gaudy pink.

* Cinderella, too, had received this pedlar on her doorstep, and squandered household money earmarked for a tapenade on a bottle of perfume, also of the Emily D. collection, "avouched to rouse the slumbering beast in even the most benumbed or befuddled bridegroom," called Sweet Wolf Within. She went on to promise that if he'd pass by again, she'd buy a foot cream that quite tickled her fancy—Doom's Electric Moccasin.

Mood

(from *The Glass Shoe*)

The prince wore a jacket that looked like ironed milk, but I was in a wrinkled linen mood. My mouth was full of easy vowels and lagging answers, and I stared long into my demitasse after finishing off a Turkish coffee: women's bodies brimming with child, mountains shaggy with fur. I don't want to end up as one of those women who cry themselves to sleep at night over a mismatched life. The prince is very nice, not at all standoffish or anything; his crown has obviously not gone to his head, and even though he's an only child raised with a silver spoon in his nanny's right hand, and tutors in German,

Greek, Italian, English, Russian, and French lisping and spluttering and sibilating at his elbow, and has had little girls all over the realm falling at his dashing feet from the day he stopped crawling, I find him kind, considerate, capable of crossing over into a woman's feelings and anticipating and fulfilling her needs before she even knows what they are herself . . . and yet I never break into slivers of astonishment over the fact that there he is, beside me, in all his fine skin and raiment, at once annihilating me, the éclat of his presence bringing me crashing to the floor like the vase I broke the other day as I was dusting around the M's in the library (Maugham, Monrós, Marias), and then scooping me up and completing me in the very depths of my demise. Oh, sure, he's a good dancer, and can converse on any number of trivial or serious matters, keeping the corners of my lips curled with amusement or my forehead crinkled in concentration, but when I come home and shrug off my clothes and tuck myself in between my own familiar humble covers, I am ravaged with ennui, and start chewing on the sheets. Perhaps something has been bred out of this boy. So I thought the other day, wondering where is the ache my heart desires:

> And what manner of beast might you once have been? A hideous creature has been enchanted and turned into a shiny prince. Its only wish: to get back its horns and scabs and slink back into the muck whence it was wrenched.

My elastic good fortune, snapping me in the face.

M O O D

"like ironed milk"
She drones on with a recitative of her responsibilities for "this gaggle of females called home" in the letter to her father that twines and whines through the diary:

"And then, after I've got a healthy roar going in the fireplace and have dropped several knives on my feet, I have to put out the milk bottles and rub down the front steps.[1] It's astonishing how much milk this household goes through in a single typical day, but they do lower their splendid abundances into bathtubs of it and splash and purr like kittens, sop up saucers of the stuff with Café Noir cookies and honeybuns at tea, and after dinner souse apple tarts or pear-and-apricot cobblers[2] in clabbered milk—their idea of a just dessert. It really is too bad you didn't stick around long enough to enjoy your own daughter's culinary talents in bloom!"

[1] In other moods on two unconnected days, the steps take part in a metaphoric descent—"Down the steps of consternation!"— and become the subject of grisly speculation: "I have often wondered if this bejowled old broad* is called my stepmother because my real mother is buried beneath the steps, and we have to step over her to get into her house."

[2] Not the same cobbler who distracted Red Shoes from her torments, although he *is* referred to in one passage as "a rustic *délice* smelling of leather and plum trees."

* What a rich store of description the diary leaves us with! There's this semiprecious glimpse of the ugly stepmother at the ball; as you will notice, Cinderella had sobriquets of her own:

"And there was Mamaliga, her jowls wagging back and forth, rhinestone earrings like bawdy chips off fallen stars slapping the aspic flesh while she boogied and batted her eyelashes at a gouty pharmacist."

"in between my own familiar humble covers"
The covers of this book.

Moon

Her face brushes across a surrendering sea.
"Call me in the evening," she says, "my
appointment book is on fire."

M O O N

"my appointment book is on fire"
Her lunarcyclical schedule of rendezvous may have found its
way (after the mugging on rue du Roi de Sicile, note to the
fragile FACE) into Yolanta's electrical appliance heating up in
note to BREAD.

Mouth

Morpheus, I do keep wondering about these scratch-
marks crossing over from those hands I know, talking to
me like that, just asking for questions burning in the
mouth of every answer I haven't given you yet.

M O U T H

"just asking for questions"
In the mock dialogue of *Carnal Knowledge*, where love
triumphs over a reductio ad absurdum and is at one point
reviled as "nothing more than the philosophical consequence
of the body's arguments," we find:

> "Because, you gorgeous dingbat, you don't belong in
> the mouth of every question ever posed."

Cf. the ingenue at the distressing threshold of DOOR: "Hey,
I don't go around jumping into just anybody's mouth!"

Mud

Her tongue scalded from the cup of cocoa and her mind filled with terrors of the tale she had just laid aside, she tossed fitfully among the bedclothes while mummies masquerading as hieroglyphs packed her, lace nightie and all, into the silt of the riverbank and spelled out her destiny in an awkward performance of calisthenics as her eyes peeped in fright from the mud.

M U D

The contents of this nightmare are understandable if one assumes that the tale she'd been disturbing herself with was "The Mauled Scribe."

Mug

(from *The Unfinished Cookie*)

Time is the mother and mugger
of us all.

Mug

He drank deeply of her mug
of reconciliation.

M U G

"deeply of her mug"
Because he and she were twin souls, and suffered one another's admiration with mixed feelings, there was a Russian

proverb,* "Do not chafe at the looking glass if your mug is awry," she was fond of quoting when he mistook some ambiguous arrangement of her features and skulked off to her boudoir to ponder the surfaces of his own.

* Never one to repeat herself, she varied this with as much invention as she could muster, producing improvisations such as:

"Do not spit in your mind's eye while gargling the malentendus of yesteryear";

"Fais pas la gueule devant la vitrine où se reposent les sous-vêtements de votre belle-mère";

and once, while waxing her own mustache,

"Quaver not before your mirror lisping, 'You're gorgeous,' fingering your lips, your greased moon of a face, tasting glass as your tongue laps reflection of rouge and jaw, if they are streaked with tears."

* "Don't make faces in front of a display window where your mother-in-law's underwear is sleeping."

Mug

Grüsse Gott! At the Eis-Café in Baden-Baden, where my blond sylphic immensity feels slightly more at home than the last place you heard me from. My cup runneth over with essentials (just cashed a traveler's check), and my mug is frothing over with excitement: I'm fresh from snow falling into gushing bowls of radioactive waters among *somnambules* of various large red sizes bobbing up and down and sinking further into flesh—the same ones who might be seen here morning or afternoon spooning foam into mouths beneath fur hats or newspapers and the frown of the German soul which seems to be saying, "There's no rest for the wicked, und zoo feeling arbeiter for the good." On the wall, four girls, seasonal tableaux, tilt their bosoms over the four gentlemen, at their separate tables, digging into *Schlag* and dragging on cigarettes. Autumn's belly opening beneath pumpkin breasts; Spring, in pale green gossamer, squats in a field of Neapolitan blooms—pink petals edged with chocolate and white—and surrounds one branch with her thighs, pulls another to her lips. Must go see if I can replace the little strip of leather that broke off my boot yesterday on the hotel stairway and was carried off by the Park-Villa bulldog, whose paws have more than once found my handknit skirt. Ah, these carbonated muscles, this tingling, fizzing skin! *Das ist alles—alles fur Nicht*, if there's no letter from you in Paris in a few weeks.

Yolanta

M U G

"my cup runneth over"

Somewhat more prosperous than during "my *Les Misérables* times," Yolanta was not in Baden-Baden to lose her royalties at the blackjack tables of its opulent casino, but to consult a physician of extraordinary intuitive powers about "a commotion in my disconnective tissue," and to take the famous cure.

"my handknit skirt"

It *was* a fetching little number an editor in New York had sent her two days after lunch at a French bistro called Tout-Va-Bien, where things went well enough through the steamed mussels and *crème caramel* once he'd poured a glass of white wine into her lap while pulling out her chair. But chic she was not (see PAJAMAS), and as for all those other things they were saying about her—"Fictions, my dear—mummery tissue," as she dismissed them in one interview.

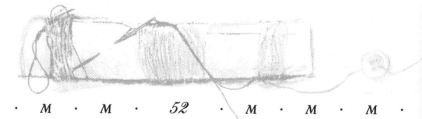

Music

He at last found out she was a piece
of sheet music anyone could play.

M U S I C

"a piece of sheet music"

That unhappy discovery was not made in Jacob Other's
Winged Sheets, but is a caption in a coloring book* of Cinderella's called *Loose Women and Tight Corners*, a take-off on
Little Women and Bright Corners, which had been a manual
for new brides in her mother's day on the way to a man's
heart ("go straight for fifty years and then take a turn for the
worse") and "brightening the corner and staying there."

* This coloring book of women with two heads and double lives,
their garments awrithe with ribbons to color in somber and scan-
dalous shades, is the only thing our girl ever shoplifted (she slipped
it beneath her camisole) in all those days of haggling, snapping
green beans, sniffing melons, and sticking out her tongue so the
Armenian cheese man could lay slivers of Kasseri, Mimolette, and
Provolone upon it and feast his eyes on the felicities invading her
features while his wife in the back room lifted crates and moaned.

Music

(from *Peter Quince at the Clavicles*)

He pounded upon her ill-tempered clavicles
with a bacchanalian bravado that calmed his
seething soul.

M U S I C

"with a . . . bravado"

A bra worn by a bullfighter. When she had first met him, she
spoke ardently of "that flagging, bright, rustling bravado he
has," and fingered her own lingerie with fresh disdain.

In *Frangipani's Pajamas*, Armada and Flotilla spend an uproarious afternoon in a Barcelona boutique trying on knickers and bravados.

Pain

(from *Life in the Forest Sauvage*)

Would the endorphins *never* come?

Perfume

PARFUM DES DEUX MAGOTS

Because her existence *was* her essence, he reduced her to it and bottled it and wore it splashed, with studied casualness, over his anomie as he dragged the boulevards.

Pillows

Among pillows of this very kind, lost souls could fluff up their sagging spirits in their waking hours, and find their bodies once again in dreams.

Pizza

I was in a Chinese restaurant.
Everyone was eating pizza.

P I Z Z A

One of Yolanta's alienation dreams, from the same rough time, or roughly the same time, as her "La dame aux échecs" phase:

Dream of my life as a chess game. Each time a piece moves into a new square, I hear it mutter, *"Merde!"*

Place

Aimless wandering can lead directly to a kind of roughhouse. It is a large, sprawling, boisterous, and absolutely wonderful place. This repulses many people seeking an easier way to their sandwiches.

P L A C E

"a kind of roughhouse"
The tavern a day's eastward journey from Plzeń you will arrive in shortly without your fairy tale T-shirt was also very noisy, with so many different native tongues loosened by every alcoholic concoction dreamed up on either side of the Danube flapping at once; and served no sandwiches, but meat, cabbage, potatoes, paprika, and onions combined in more ways than seems possible to our jaded palates. The blind innkeeper Frantisek, an autodidactic polyglot, stood around jawing with the customers while his formidable wife Katja, a woman of phenomenal constitution and mandibles, ran the whole show, giving birth at dawn to one baby after another till they numbered thirteen, slaughtering oxen in the noontime sun, dealing with the peasants who supplied what food they didn't raise themselves, supervising the airing of the linens from the second-story windows, keeping an eye out for pickpockets in the smoky den of iniquity the hostel might at any moment become, and still found the time, energy, and maternal instinct to tell the bashful servant girl to take her fingers out of her mouth.

Place

(from *The Gingerbread Variations*)

ARRIVAL FOR FOUR VOICES:

> I think we're in the wrong place.
> I'm just glad we found it.
> I hope we never leave.
> Maybe we could take it with us.

P L A C E

"Arrival for Four Voices"

Four lost children at first sight of the gingerbread house while straying through the woods. There are many fugues of similar theme in the gingerbread archives (not part of the *Lebkuchen Häuschen* canon proper), thanks to the tapes that were confiscated when the witch was burned. A true artist at heart, she had embedded a voice-activated cassette recorder in a patch of gumdrops embellishing the front gate so that she could later play back these comments of passersby and captivated little ones, take note, then give them serious consideration as she made her sketches for redoing the cake in the spring.

Rain

Torquil, I know that these all-embracing desires are just asking for trouble, that it's better to begin in the glass of water, which can shatter, spill over, be taken in to the last liquid moment, be knocked over, refilled, have something else poured in. Who knows? A rainstorm can fall into a glass, and the things that happen after the storm has passed. I wanted to add something to your life, which is not the same as replacing what isn't already there. There's the touch, clash, or fusion with each other and making something of it alone: the intensity leaps onto synapses not our own and the hunger (mine, anyway) goes out. When I give myself to you, I am suddenly everyone's woman, as anyone can see, after you've gone, if I wade out into the streets with this backwards waterfall rushing through me, from the sidewalk and my shoes. The hunger is a delight. And thank you for lunch in the dying light, your self to drape mine over in the coffee and dusk of an outdoors wider than that terrace seemed to say, for listening, for telling me. If, next time, there's anything within reach, a glass, you, I'll take it, I'll be with you, much taken, as always.

found on floor by
window: a DARK feather

Jonquil

R A I N

There must have been another man in Jonquil's life:

I thought of you.
It rained hard for one minute.
I thought of him.
The roof began to leak.

Real

**You don't think I'm not real when I'm
kidding, and you don't want to believe
I am real when I'm not.**

R E A L

"when I'm kidding"

Yolanta, having a bit of epistemological fun with the boys at
the Préfecture de Police, mugging in front of the camera,
making eyes at their superiors, and offering to show them
her tattoo instead of revealing her name.

"I am real"

As an exposition of *clitoris*, this curious image crops up in
Don Juan Is a Woman:

> A piece of real estate. The
> owner hollers in a back room.

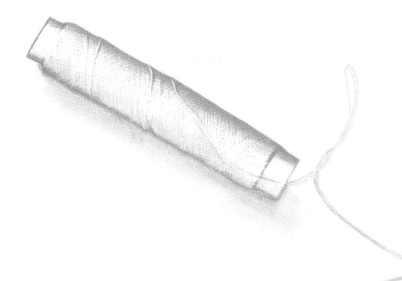

Salt

On a recent Sunday afternoon, the contents of my refrigerator included not much more than the drowsy greenness of wild ponies and a milliner, a dressmaker, a dancer, and a singer.

This was unfortunate, because when they were alive, they had run a souvenir shop in Ostend full of bric-a-brac salted with the North Sea, and skeletons warming themselves at the stove.

S A L T

"a milliner"

Before winding up in someone's Sunday brunch, she managed to complete a collection of twentieth-century literature hats (see HAT) and a big picture hat for the restless young bride in DRESS, whom she suspected of being every inch the aficionado of cheap thrills long before people started talking, and even avoiding her. Funny to find her, the milliner, in this tableau vivant of Ensor's childhood, as it was his self-portrait in plumed hat that had decided her on her calling and rescued her from those chilly studios where she posed and shivered for so little money and began so many hopeless liaisons with sensitive and penniless young men.

"a dressmaker"

No, it's not Elsbeth,* who, at the time, was rereading a postcard from Czechoslovakia that had arrived on Saturday from her niece.

* Oh, please read FROCK! You should have a long time ago. Then SCAR will make more sense.

Salt

(from *The Glass Shoe*)

By the time the *huevos rancheros* arrived at the sleepy hacienda, we had eaten enormously off the platter of sunrise, tickled the *banditti* gagged and bound in a corner of the patio, and licked the rims of salt from each other's tequila'd lips.

S A L T

"from each other's tequila'd lips"

In another splinter of the Cinderella story, she "clattered across the dusty highway through tumbleweeds in her hand-blown Mexican glass slippers." Was Cinderella at the hacienda, then, licking the wounded *banditti* and drinking margaritas from a salted glass shoe? In Venice, she wore shoes of Murano glass, and from the Bridge of Sighs on her still unsubstantiated honeymoon, saw a girl with runaway red shoes kicking a gondolier in the head.

Satin

Thinking himself home alone with his thoughts, and finding one of them painful beyond human endurance, the recluse raged among his cushions as he recalled the taste of satin and the mannequin's unclaspable *désinvolture.*

Scar

Brushing against a nail on the deck chair in which the millionaire had propped her, the dummy, no longer in diamonds and furs, but in yachting togs, and looking rather pale, scraped her muslin* kneecap, ripping it open and getting a bit of rust on her white skirt. She stared out at the Caribbean, not green like the promises—but had anything been like he'd painted it, after their first few weekends at country inns, where it had been so awkward sharing bathtubs with strangers down the hall?—and several loops of stuffing came twirling down her shin. Cotton socks, shredded libretti, and ancient manuscripts were the stuff she was made of, stories lacing through each other, sometimes getting tangled there, beneath her skin (which someone had once disdainfully or insensitively referred to as her upholstery)—about a passion in The Black Forest (sort of a Wagnerian opera but all mixed up with Greek and Roman myth, and who knows what sort of children this coupling might produce; Pan pipes, shepherds' flutes, Orpheus tiptoeing around the cypresses, but then this very *gemütlich* feeling taking over not only the amatory but also the musical theme); an Albanian having trouble with his map; and other histories from beyond that sullen sea.

Well, she would have to wait till he carried her back to their cabin before calling the seamstress, a soft-focused Croatian on holiday, to come in and read her these "scraps of the narrative handkerchief," as she called her insides, before tucking them back into the fabric of her being and apologizing for the scar this would leave.

* This made life easy, because she could do her laundry and bathe all at once, tossed into the tub, fully clothed, with some very mild soap and *cold* water, or else the colors of her eyes might bleed, and no girl would want to be seen with her irises bolting down her cheeks, or any of her other markings in places where they had no right to be.

S C A R

"no longer in diamonds and furs"

She was last seen in literature occupying a coveted seat in an opera house. Neither the same season nor city as the penguin's night out in WATCH.

"muslin"
The exalted role muslin has played in art and the warping
and woofing of language is given more elaborate treatment
in *Frangipani's Pajamas* than you are dying to let me tell you
about here.

"ancient manuscripts"
Of which a crisp page disappeared in LIPS.

"passion"
See LEGS; THING.

"irises bolting"
See BOUDOIR, where she bolts into the irises.

"apologizing for the scar this would leave"
Anja's actual words were:

> *"Posekotina je izlečena ali brazgotina se još vidi.
> Hajd, hajde, umiri se."**

* "The cut is healed but you can see the scar. There, there, my
dear."

"scraps of the narrative handkerchief"
By now it will be dawning on you what stories they are, and
where Anja happened upon all these tatters she's been piecing
together for you.

Shadow
(from *The Gingerbread Variations*)

In those days it was bitter cold when the angels talked
to a fellow at night as his shadow paused to listen for a
way out of the woods.

"Hansel, what hast thou done with thy sister?"
"Ah, scattered her bones to make the trip home
easier."

Now don't start dabbing at your eyes with your handkerchief. This was only one of Gretl's fantasies as she lay awake at night in the witch's bedroom wondering, after what she'd just been through, how their story would ever end, and took into consideration the treatment experience had taught her to expect from her brother. "Cowering at an indecent angle" is how she summed up these childhood memories of his humiliations when she was grown and had children of her own clambering over her lap.

"scattered her bones"
Sometimes passages of *The Gingerbread Variations* look like they're treading on Nichevo's toes, as in this scene for the corps de ballet:

> Lovely in verdant underwear   the callous and grizzled dandies waltz beside their bones. The timid stitch tuxedos   gamble away their siestas   mate in rotundas of gingerbread . . .

Skin

The special guest of the skeleton.

S K I N

One of the "tidings from Timofey," whiling away Eternity with his own lexicon, haunted by a line from Tarkovsky's *Nostalghia*: "To light up like a word, posthumously."

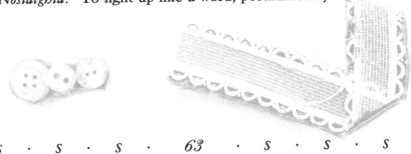

Sleep

Morpheus, your presence wraps around my past, the gift you found me in. Now that you're the present, it brushes past history and various outrageous misfortunes for the future and paints the way into the clearing where the only entanglement is ours. And even while the brim of each tiny wound dawned on me, there was somehow less pain, this time, in your love, which made me stay up outside all night after leaving you a note that said, "You've left my body purring so loudly the sound is keeping me awake." Specific sadnesses are spreading into a lazier, more vaguely inherent one. When I speak of places I want to sleep with you, it's not to summon dreams to fill in the present, which feels so full, but to catch some of the extra moments spilling over and touching on all sides others the way your touching me gives birth to *cent mille milliards de* phantom limbs

in phantom limbus,
there, where the edges are blurring,
as I had hoped we would,

K

Soup

Salut! I wandered out of my hotel this morning looking for a place to get warm, wound up at Beaubourg, whose bubbles are filled with sadness already despite the structure's youth. A distintegrated, ravaging need has rubbed against it too desperately; the brightness has been snuffed out, and only fatigue remains. Here in the Bibliothèque (a place where the homeless find chairs, or, if none are left, arrange themselves in lumps along the walls), a man beside me is mumbling to himself in Bulgarian as he heavily thumbs his way through a dictionary that looks like a thick Balkan soup. He wheezes and gasps between each word; the rest of us sharing his strange guttural dinner table exchange unknowing looks. I'll be in New York in April. See you there over a bowl of borscht at that Ukranian place by the Village Gate.

—*T'embrasse,*
Yolanta

S O U P

"through a dictionary"
Not *this* dictionary, Absinthe to Zipper, abounding though it is in Balkan ambience.

Sparkle

(from *The Little Match Girl*)

So I pulled over to the side of the
road and sparkled for a while.

Stamps

There were always a few overseas postage stamps swimming around in his sperm. His first love had been a Swedish exchange student, and he never quite got over her.

S T A M P S

Jonquil, with an airplane wing stuck to that soft spot on her innermost thigh, finally brought herself to mention to Torquil that she felt she did deserve, by their third weekend together, after all, some explanation for this phenomenon.

<h1>Stars</h1>

(from *The Little Match Girl*)

I had this silk scarf* wrapped around my face but it was damp from my tears and then frozen and so it was stuck to me in a most unpleasant way. My eyelashes were also encrusted with fresh snowflakes, each a miracle of the theretofore never expressed never to again occur, right there, on my own eyelashes—it was an awesome thought and made me more appreciate each second ticking by, for each of these, too, was like none other, no matter how long I gazed through this same pane of glass with a whiteness all around me and so much night yet to come.

* The silk scarf, a deep blue square bordered by tight metallic stars, as if the stars had been thrown out to the edge of day and were waiting to scatter over its fields once again, I found one morning on my doorstep, folded and refolded into a thick rectangle and tucked into one of my own matchboxes with a note in a large, careful, muscular hand.*

> * No, this is not one of the hands I now had tossed over my shoulder, and I might add here that it was so cold—maybe this will give you some idea of how cold it *was*—that I wanted to cover my fur hands with gloves. One by one I took them into my own hands and rubbed them and breathed on them just as the man I buy my vegetables from once did with mine* when my blue hand held out to him a coin in exchange for some leeks and potatoes I intended to glorify in a shepherd's pie.
>
>> * This is one of the most touching things anyone has ever done for me, perhaps because it was so immediate a response to a very real condition. It wasn't as if he had been staying awake for nights wondering what he could possibly do for that wretched creature robbed of her girlhood by poverty and a father who punished her with or for his own sorry lot and self-hatred—and I smiled up gratefully at him with all my being as it engulfed his warmth.

Table

She sat at a small round flat cracked marble table with too many adjectives around her in one of those cafés by the sea.

T A B L E

Parts of this cracked table have been lost, but some intermittent sentences were retrieved before the demitasses and glasses of water were cleared away:

> Across the street a cement mixer grinding out its thick song. Someone, who sounded like a man, chuckled to himself on the radio, and a chorus of female voices behind him confirmed his private, loudspeakered mirth. . . . The coffee came, and with it the waitress's legs and halfhearted hopes for a decent tip . . . She waited for the coffee to cool, playing up the Nolo Me Tangere of the unaccompanied woman with an exaggerated absorption in her book . . . All this took place under the gaze of a perfect stranger sitting two tables away. Strangers are always so perfect, she sighed, until they strike the first match, until they face up to the menu, until they see what a bitch I am.

Table

Like corners torn from four other tables, they would come together for dinner to rub their ragged edges across each other over bowls of bubbling *ragoût*, glasses of not so spritely Beaujolais, and tales of their childhoods they could never finish because there was nothing for dessert.

Teeth

(from *The Gingerbread Variations*)

Eyes darted like nervous beads in the hazel bushes and traced glints of small animal appetites over the forest bed, and the lost children breathed softly through scenes of squeaking carnage, sharp teeth ripping into fine sinews, the crunch of tiny bones. The beast of dawn did come at last and put an end to all this slaughter, bringing with him the more relaxed chomping sounds of herbivores, and low-slung quadrupeds who rummaged among the scrubby foliage for nuts and seeds and dense little fruits. Bees appeared from nowhere and stuck their feet into newly opened flowers, brushed them off on the doormats of others, returning still dusty with pollen to the hives that belonged to the odd, tall woman with hair like honey and an outrageous outfit she donned to plunder the golden centers of their glutinous homes.

Long past dawn slept Hansel and Gretl, until the sun had risen high above the chirring trees, warming the earth and the two entwined bodies growling with hunger for berries, hot muffins, and fresh cream. But they had hours of famished stumbling to get through before the fateful stuffing with scented cakes.

T E E T H

"breathed softly"

This implies a long night of uninterrupted sound sleep, and it wasn't that way for Gretl at all. For hours they had followed a very talkative stream in and out of shadows and sunlight, and she had repeatedly lowered her muzzle into the current to guzzle its delightful waters and watch spiders skating across her reflected face, bits of twig or leaf riding over her eyebrows and cheeks. So all through the night and early morning she kept having to lift Hansel's arm from around her waist, lay it gently down, and get up to pee in the moonlight flowing over them "like Walter de la Mare's undershirt," she thought the first time she had awakened in this lovely embrace, snug as two gingerbread cookies fresh from the oven and wrapped in a napkin of affection, or a dishtowel of necessity.

Telephone

**"You're wanted on the other
end of my whine."**

T E L E P H O N E

"my whine"
She also sulked, howled, whimpered, trilled: his importunate mistress on Torquil's answering machine.

Aside from his menacing promenades, the only thing a bit strange about the man in the red cape was his conviction that Mozart was leaving messages on *his* answering machine.

Telephone

**"Oh, sorry—I thought you were someone else."
"Ah, yes, I had hoped so too."**

T E L E P H O N E

"someone else"
From *The Wronged Number.*
    Allusions in Jacob Other's writings repeatedly graze their lips over that extra person he carries around in his name. The preface to his collection of essays *Couplets and Breasts* demurs: "I am a man of letters, but I am a woman of something worse."

Telephone

"How's it going?"
"Fine, as long as it keeps its distance from me."

"Who are you to understand?"
"Who are you to not be understood?"

"Well, bye-bye."
"I never really hang up."
"I never really call."

T E L E P H O N E

A couple of the regulars of the torn TABLE ("We sat around chomping on platitudes"*) indulging in a meaningful mid-morning chat.

* Whereas, in *Carnal Knowledge*, "we got the machinery in motion for a perfectly desultory evening of carnal non sequiturs."

Thing

Bathed in moonlight and soaked in schmaltz, Hilda lay in his arms (or should she call them his legs?) on the forest floor, crooning lieder and popping gooseberries into his mouth and telling him fairy tales from her childhood, of the little girl who sold her grandmother for a pot of cream and grew into a fur coat. What a gratified big girl *she* was—the clever things he could do with his cloven hoofs!

Time

Dear Torquil,

Now I have your clock. Is this your answer to "I want to be the time you have on your hands"? You've left your time in mine. The hands haven't stopped moving yet.

Love,
Jonquil

Time

Someone is watching you
strapped to the back of
your life.

T I M E

Another of the entries from beyond the grave in Timosha's pocket dictionary. See skeletons with POCKETS, Yolanta's double-entendu London dream. There is cause for conjecture that something was gnawing at the bones of his departed conscience; under *remorse* we find: "Stacked up like laundry in hell."

Toothbrush

(from *The Telltale Toothbrush*)

It was the time of Dentyne, a time when all you wanted was a pair of clean teeth, and many, even women, could not brush after every meal.

"There's nothing personal about my life.
Lay off my toothbrush, you creep."

Toothbrush

(from *The Glass Shoe*)

I know I've been difficult, obstinate, irascible, recalcitrant, and hardly ever nice, but how else can I behave, in accordance with the laws of my heart? I should never see the prince again, as I think he, too, understood tonight in the shattered smile I turned on him when he left me at my door. What the door was in the act of disclosing: my disappearance from his side. Yes, I wanted him to leave me here. It was apparent how things would go this evening from the moment he handed me the orchids and I said, "Thanks, I'll brush my teeth with them," and stuck them in a jug above the bathroom sink. During dinner he kept laying his napkin over my hands and then humping them with his and drinking from my glass. He assured me that he loved me absolutely and without conditions, and I listened respectfully and, with grave doubts, smashed my meringue with the back of his spoon.

Torte

I've been torted!

The chalet we had rented in the Zillertal turned out to be haunted by a Viennese pastry chef and we had to change our plans, so we crossed over the Dolomites and continued on to Bled. It was awful! About two or three o'clock we'd be awakened by the scents of chocolate and raspberries whooshing over the eiderdown, and then a snuffling sound, followed by lips smacking and a soft groan of gustatory pleasure, would be emitted not far from our bed. Well, you can just imagine the paroxysms of terror and desire this sent us into night after night. Running out of room, these damn postcards, see you in late August, bye for now. Aren't these cobblestone streets cute? Ha! Ask my D'Orsay pumps about that!

Yolanta

Touch

"Does that feel good?"
"It's putting a small dent
in my misfortune."

T O U C H

"a small dent"

This comeback to Torquil some time between breakfast and bed during a holiday tryst recalls Jonquil's cycle of autoerotic poems, starting in a 1953 Thunderbird and grinding to a halt on a taxi ride through Central Park—particularly one titled "Trade":

> We're in the auto trade.
> He masturbates while I bang
> out his dents.

It's a reversal of the actual proposition she refused: a guy comes to her door offering to do some body work on the battered black Peugeot in front of her house in exchange for—well, he just stands there exposing her to himself with an omnivoraciously lowering gaze.

There *is* something to be said for doorways, front porches, and steps. In *The Glass Shoe*, not only the dwarf with his bag of boar bristles, but murmurs like this in the notebook beside Cinderella's bed:

> "It was definitely a day to lie about on one's doorstep, licking one's wounds or one's lollipop."

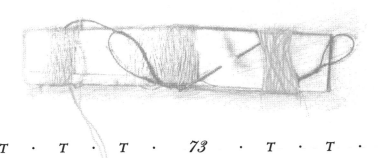

Towel

(from *The Toes of Nichevo*)

> It pattered about the room indiscreetly,
> calling for sausages, beer, a towel to dry
> its feet.

T   O   W   E   L

The Toes of Nichevo

Originally presented as a ballet, then as a radio play.

Not all the terpsichorean quality was sacrificed in this rendering for the BBC. The ballet was translated into poetic language by Yolanta, who was hard up for money in London at the time.

> The oldest puppeteer hastens me to his gristle.
> Alone we enter the discothèque of the shoeshine
> of the moon. Alone we dance.

And much more of the same sort of stuff.

Towel

Oh, how she loved to stand about the lobby of an afternoon, nabbing at passersby with her chronic cheerfulness, snapping her bright voice at them like a towel!

T   O   W   E   L

"snapping her bright voice"

Her daughter had to send her to Switzerland, where she became one of the hypochondriac's reasons for checking out so soon.

From Timofey, glossing over nothing in his amaranthine alphabet:

> What are tears?
> Lock your face in a
> closet full of towels.

Truffle

(from *Life in the Forest Sauvage*, Chapter 14: "The Truffled Pig")

There was once a large adolescent male pig who had been trained since sucklinghood practically to hunt truffles in the forest in France of course. Life was not pleasant for this pig, who was mostly black with some large white elliptical spots, for he was often beaten by the truffle merchants. They were a rude, swarthy bunch with gruff voices and unendearing ways. They weren't even nice to women. They always carried large tree branches and gave the pig sound swats on his handsome mottled back and his dusty flanks. His flanks were dusty from his work in the forest, and his snout was a caked mess of dank earth gone dry in the sharp autumn air. The pig was not exactly unhappy, or so he preferred to think of it, but one day more than usually brilliant with white-and-blue slow motion and glints off evergreens, he took his snout out of the ground long enough to start wandering through a particularly beguiling section of woods, and happened before long upon a hut like the Baba Yaga houses in Russian fairy tales: that is, it stood on legs, chicken legs, and turned on them, and this house talked to itself sometimes. Well, wouldn't you? Out the front door, which was not exactly closed, came an old man on skinny legs that looked like they were running even when he was walking quite slowly. He wore a long white T-shirt with variegated spots on it and that was all, had wild hair and rosy cheeks. The pig, having read Edith Sitwell on English eccentrics, recognized him straight off as a hermit, and not the kind you chain to a rock beyond your back door. The hermit, who sometimes called himself Henri, welcomed the pig with unencroaching glee and made it quite clear with few words and many gestures that he might make his home there. True harmony came easily once the pig routed out a place for himself and recounted his sordid tale. The hermit goes on with his quiet life, reading movie magazines and writing fan letters to his favorite stars, and the pig is free to roam the forest with his nose in the air and eat the hermit's cassoulet, to which, when he's feeling like it, he occasionally contributes a truffle.

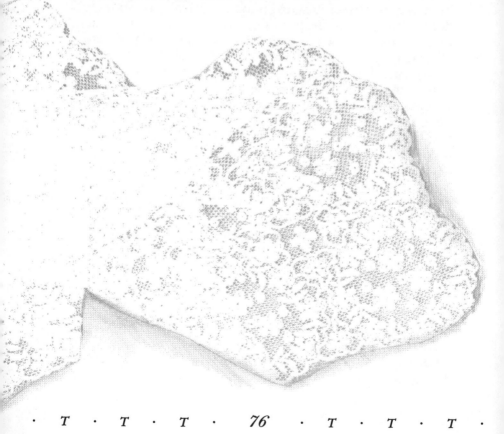

Wall

On her way back from the doorstep of death, she paused to consider biting the wall.

W A L L

All she'd really been after was "a complete rest from the worst of life for the better part of the time," her suicide note said. The wall wasn't even made of gingerbread, so she had second thoughts about that, too.

Jacob Other amplifies this interpretation *and* suggests an alternate reading:

> "She" is a little playmate of the Girl Next Door (see the final DOOR), and a precocious purveyor of Girl Scout cookies who'd read Kafka's *Hunger Artist* at an impressionable age; or this same child was simply skipping home from her chum's, her stomach growling, after an afternoon of Little Richard, Buddy Holly, and "Chantilly Lace."

Watch

(from *The Little Match Girl*)

I took one of the fur hands into my own and held it by the wrist to read its pulse. The loud ticking of the Swatch watch I'd bought on the rue de Rivoli was distracting, mixing its ticks up with the beat of the blood, so I pressed its face against my back and muffled it in my coat. The beat seemed sluggish to me, but I don't know how to correlate these things with blood pressure, metabolic changes in subzero temperatures, degrees of wakefulness, and the presence of light, of which we have so little in this circumpolar region. I do recall once hearing about the grim struggles of the penguin to keep his metabolism intact, and the picture of his life painted against that blasting white background did much to allay my misimpression about the intrinsic comicalness of these birds, and affected my feelings about the amusing behavior of one of our *enfants terribles* at the Opéra. Not wishing to wear tails himself one night, he appeared in his box with a penguin at his side, shifting it to his knees after the entr'acte, and cradling the sleepy Sphenicada in his arms through the final scenes of *La Bohème*, for the barblessly feathered visitor was overwhelmed by the warmth thrown off from tiers of bejeweled torsos emerging from fur wraps and heavy scents and curls.

W A T C H

"and heavy scents"

The penguin was not put off by scented or bejeweled torsos per se. *Au contraire*, one of his most ardent pursuits those first euphoric few weeks in Paris had been waddling around the Faubourg St. Honoré with a lady friend who permitted him, *"avec plaisir, chéri,"* to atomize her pulse points with his own selections, bending over his shiny black head or holding him up to her throat and listening to his cries of approval or disbelief. So, this evening at the Opéra, before the mélange drove him completely out of his senses, he was able to distinguish, with the satisfaction of the budding connoisseur, such fragrances as Demimonde, Fleurs du Malheur, Grosse Bête, Perdition, Flagrante Delicto, and a new one called Mazeltov that was making a big splash in the heat of the Dreyfus Affair.

Wind

Just back to London by Deux Chevaux (home to a garden shutting down for the winter, the furniture put away under plastic, and one lonely hollyhock flower violetly nodding its head over things going to seed) from two weeks on the coast of Cornwall, a twelve-hour trip in the little red truck, with a stop at Castle Drogo (Lutyens, pre-New Delhi) and a visit to a Medieval manor, Montacute, now in the tweedy hands of the National Trust—followed by a Devon cream tea that ruined dinner for the next two weeks (well, that's laying it on a bit thick). London looks positively festive with its cars and red and green lights, shop and pub signs, and its roundabouts about which Londoners so courteously comport themselves. Sunday afternoon, today, we strolled among other ones on foot in Kew Gardens, where they were out catching the autumn light, and trees were burnished in red and god (gold, but the typo stays).

In Cornwall we wandered around the countryside, had to stop at every church, named for saints like Issy, Petherick, Columba (a fifteen-year-old who saved her village from a bear), and in every town and village, each with its curious pattern of streets; and everywhere my head was blasted through by winds, rains, clouds, some hot sunshine (during a ten-mile hike along disappeared railroad tracks and through fields each with the obligatory disquieting bull, and one pub for a Smuggler's Split a brief road offered up before we clambered over another wall), the sound of relentless Atlantic waves whipped up and dashing against the rocks.

We slept like two muffins in a toaster (the caravan on Treyarnon Bay was not much bigger than one), and when it rained, I curled up with radio plays on the BBC, Boswell's *Life of Johnson*, Cornish ghost stories, and the weekly newspaper, mostly about cows. Even the one crime reported came out MILK BOTTLE USED AS DEADLY WEAPON. Went to a horse auction to look at the animals and people—wild-eyed ponies, and country types with broad high cheekbones stuffing Cornish pasties into their mouths. You can walk for days along the coast, at cliff-edge, on the softest, greenest turf (just ask my bare feet, not deprived of this tactile thrill), over footpaths that have been padded upon for generations of pirates and dairymen. We lived on mushrooms picked every other day in a cow field near Bedruthan's Steps (Bedruthan was a giant who stalked through here centuries ago; his steps lead down to the sea, where once his large footprints were lapped away), crab, mussels, sea spinach growing savagely along every wall and hedge, clotted cream, toast and marmalade, and all that clean fierce air.

Yolanta

Window

She lived to open closed letters, and to
loop each word through its other windows,
out of the worlds within.

W I N D O W

See the painted envelope of whispers flying off on a carpet from DOOR into the next volume of the dummy's tales.

The window next to this one was written for Sylvia Monrós-Stojaković, whose borzoi letter Anja quotes in her correspondence with Elsbeth: ". . . they run in circles around the wolf trying desperately to run away in a straight line." See also the alarming wave in note to DRESS. And the little match girl's footsteps delivering her again and again to the wolf at the window of her death. But Anja was discussing the art of tidy seams.

Closet
Drama

We had our debacles to rehearse,
our shortcomings to undress

Babushka

"Here, they just didn't get dry enough," he said with concern for her warfare as he dabbed at her tears with a corner of her own babushka, which could also turn into a flour sack* should the shortage of occasion demand.

* Usually it was a fine buckwheat flour, for blini were popular in her movable household of men, women, and children dangling from her apron, and pots and pans clanging against their helmets and bulletproof vests.*

  * Not versts, which they traveled many of sometimes of a day; of others, they might not stray far from the sizzling butter, the sour cream, and the caviar* beside a river flowing off the page ·   .

  * The caviar, it must be noted, was a matter of robbery, for the routes they followed were those of the Beluga merchants and not of Chichikov.*

    * Just picture this one as the flapping of an inside-out overcoat whose lining, empty of any particular soul, could propel his droshky around a Mother Russia no one had ever swerved through, breaking off whole chapters of a novel-in-progress as count less talented and invisible serfs fell into the .

B A B U S H K A

They camped out in pockets of the Motherland's big apron.

Belt

(from *The Red Shoes*)

What could she do but lavish attention on them, accursed though they might be? She bought a red leather purse and belt to match them, a pleated hound's-tooth skirt. She polished and buffed them, smoothed over each scuff as well as she could; and when they needed resoling or were down at the heels, she wore them to the cobbler's and spent the night there if he couldn't get to them right away. Every year she sent the cobbler a greeting card on St. Crispin's Day, a gesture that never occurred to his other customers, and she wore galoshes when it rained.

B E L T

In Ingmar Bergman's film* of *The Red Shoes*, they (Liv, Erland, Bibi, even Sven) are wearing scratchy scarves and distressing shoes, and are expressing lots of angst. After the movie, a kiosk opens in the lobby so that members of the audience can buy their very own red shoes and then have something to point to in their woes and sufferings. See PAIN.

* Bergman's films also figure in this virgin-spring-and-allish sequel to the patisserisqué foreplay of JAR:

> He stretched out her shortcake, he tamed her wild strawberries, he was her smiles of a summer knight in blinding ardor.

Bodice

As the pale author banged out pastoral prose in her darkened chamber on the conjugal bed, her impostor scampered among the nasturtiums, crunching the delightful papery flames of their petals and the peppery leaves, rolling in them, running them through her fingers, and stuffing them into her bodice swollen with abundance and greed.

Boots

The foxholes were all full, and I was naked, alone, and alarmed. Shots swam past me in slow motion. I was the missing mark. Beneath my footfalls lay the best of bargains: terra firma, half dead or asleep. My boots were muddy, my face was a mess, but I was too cold to care, and why should I look any better in a rifle's line of sight? I was glad I'd chosen the First World War to be in because it was easier then to get around on foot, and I could speak a little French. In the trench. I looked around for my buddies but they were neither dead nor alive and so I sat around waiting for my brother who was born after the Second World War, two years ahead of me, because I was fighting before my time had come.

B O O T S

"my boots were muddy"

During another, less metaphorical visit in France (the reverie is from her bestiary), Yolanta ate her way through the back streets of Paris ("off the eaten path") for the book *A Crusty Baguette, a Cup of Beaujolais*:

> Last night I walked down rue de Bellechasse to La Sologne, a restaurant that chose the right street, for everything they serve once ran wild—little birds brought together into *confits*, small furred creatures I couldn't translate into English or back to life, grouse, *morilles*, berries, forest seeds. The place was rather like a lodge in the woods, and the welcome as if I were knocking the mud off my boots and hanging up my shotgun to tuck in for a bit of warmth in the dark winter's night. And so the bright berries and *cheminée*. Once before, while ogling the young deer in bitter chocolate at the adjoining table, and three tiny American children tend-

ing to their *plats* with interest, then to their mousses with lust, I dined on wild baby boar in a light, tangy sauce with bacon, mushrooms, over fresh pasta in two colors and surrounded by a ruby ring of fresh cranberries. Last night, though, no craving to sink my teeth into savage flesh, so I had several hors d'oeuvres, delicate, dusky mixtures of wild vegetables and herbs, and, well, one bone to toss to the carnivore in me, a bed of spinach and herbs with thin slices of white pheasant meat.

Boots

(from *The Little Match Girl*)

My Russian grandmother sat in the corner with her red boots listening to the wolves.

B O O T S

"My Russian grandmother"

Vasilisa, who, in her younger days, loved to bully her husband Vanya by making him eat much more kasha than he wanted and by taking up the choicest spot in their house on the steppes. He would come home with his ax to find her flattened out on the stove whose belly he had been out finding provisions for, as he would be on the following day, too, and every day of the long winter that came and went year after year. As the howling wolves announce more eloquently than a bit of crepe sewn to the edge of the page, this booted baba is one of the last grandmas in the little match girl's hallucinations brought on by hunger and the approach of death. Vasilisa, her red boots comfortably propped on a low table groaning with zakuski,* comes hard on the heels of a tough old Serb with paprikas strung over her shoulders and blisters on her feet; grandmothers with fingers stained from turmeric, raspberries, and Turkish cigarettes; grandmothers in yashmaks, sarongs, kimonos, negligées; and a Betty Crocker grandmother, her apron dusted with flour, grieving for the unfinished cookie, and up to her elbows in chopped walnuts and chocolate chips.

* Oh, God, I wish I were eating
  some right now!

Bra

I say! How can I excite you to these raptures regarding the celestial machine, that mechanical angel duck, that brought me here from Boulogne, skim you along all the sensory impressions playing on me since my arrival ("She longed to go to England, to the land of Christopher Smart, to inhale the noxious vapours that nourished his exalted soul")? Looks in the streets of London are furtive, disarming after the outright unwrappings a woman undergoes in Paris—I used to walk out of a *métro* car fumbling at my buttons and the hook of my bra strap, so surely did they feel undone, so shimmeringly did I sometimes feel sated of a steamy afternoon (name of *métro* line: Erotic Transport)—but my eyes are agog here, anyway, watching, for one thing, streets changing their names in the middle of puddles (yesterday I went on a Plague Walk), and sounds, too, have struck me, like the footsteps, with clipped, working-class accents, leaving for home at five o'clock. At night, the rumble of trains in Waterloo Station rattles the window where I sleep, and I half expect to wake up one morning halfway to Scotland in a bed of damp heather beside a track of British Rail. Must get gussied up in a hurry and start queuing up in the West End. By God, I believe this *is* the time I imagine I'm having!

Love,
Yolanta

Button

She buttoned up the house, folded it, stuffed it into her purse, locking the front door, and entered the foot traffic flowing past the secret dwelling no mugger would ever guess she now had clenched in her fist.

B U T T O N

"folded it"

See also STARS, SHIRT, WEDDING TRAIN, and note to SLIP. And KIMONO, turning a body inside out.

In the carnival scene of *The Toes of Nichevo* we have:

> Hard on the heels of the pickpocket came a button collector through the crowd.

The part of the button collector was danced by Poco Rabinowitz, who in MACARONI plays himself, a faun in camouflage rolling his eyes while the nymph, a friend of Effie's named Strophe, strips the surrounding foliage of vegetal parasites for the ongoing cosmetic experiments that so absorb the nymphs in their streams and glades.

Cap

She knitted a loud woolen cap of her recriminations and yanked it over his head.

C A P

She was already wearing a piece of silly headgear, I guess (well, *someone* has to keep the milliner in grub and finery), because the scene continues:

> "You're not miffed, are you?" he asked, taking a cautious peep into her bonnet as a bank of nimbus clouds rolled forth from its brim.

Cape

The man in the red cape put on Mozart's Divertimento in D Major (K. 136), rummaged around in his sewing basket for a spool of scarlet thread, made a double *Kaffee mit Schlag*, and, as St. Martin gamboled about in the melodic fields, addressed himself to the fraying matter of his hood.

C A P E

One of many quiet moments with himself when he's not out stalking and frightening little girls, or is it sturdy *Hausfrauen* he pursues? Tenderly domestic and very particular about the arrangement of his cottage, his recordings of Mozart and Schubert, the laundering of his shirts hanging all over the place to dry. Rather full around the hips. Just enough to affect his movements, the swish of his cape. Never short of invitations. See PELISSE.

Coat

A fine coat of lust lay over every thoughtful surface of the room.

C O A T

This could be either Cinderella, out of her DRAWERS, or Jonquil, thinking of love as "a little adventure looking for the right surface to happen upon" and "stretching myself out, in case someone wants to leave a message plastered to my body."

Coat

"The Asinine Menagerie" is puzzling: a reworking of a La Fontaine (misspelled here, however, for some reason, as La Fontagne—I don't know about this girl's French, or was she dreaming of Chamonix?) fable, with the animals all transported to the Arctic North and wearing coats made of other animals' fur.

C O A T

"The Asinine Menagerie"
Another review by Jacob Other. Always short. "Form follows malfunction," Jacob says, pointing to his bad back and the curtness of his own critical style. His one essay on visual art produced the epigram "Art is only abstract when you look the other way."

Collar

(from *The Red Shoes*)

The silhouette was jerking its head and munching its collar as its coach rolled past Daphne's darkened door.

COLLAR

Anja didn't much care to take in work from apparitions, shadows, and other nebulous beings, but this one was so lightweight and mild-mannered, except for a fervent feeling about sound sartorial sensuousness, and a profound respect for her craft, and came the first time with his own sketch of the shirt he wanted, including some elaborate notions about the collar* to hide a birthmark at his throat, that Anja accepted the wad of dinars he pressed into her palm and agreed to the rest of his reasonable terms.

* The same collar, perhaps, that turns up in Elsbeth's painterly portrait of her still unseen, faceless friend: "Anja took a pin out of her mouth and jabbed it into a collar that lay in a curve in her lap. The rays of a setting sun caught on the edge of a silver box containing buttons and snaps and a lozenge for last winter's sore throat."*

    * See note to SCARF.

Crown

(from *The Glass Shoe*)

Leaving her crown of thorns with the hat-check girl, she slipped into her carapace and slithered across the parquet floor till she arrived at his pigskin toes.

Dress

She was the daughter of a shopkeeper and was married off to a peasant, a downcast peasant with white bread. All her things were carted uphill to his house and she was put in her place. But not for long! She sat for a while on a train beside her husband. He returned to his plowing and sowing and rubbing his roughened hands on his pants. She would go to the beach alone in a long white dress and a big picture hat and watch the waves. She'd watch and wait for a long time in the fog or sun, and when she saw a wild one coming, she'd go out to meet it, and that tumbling suction roaring her under and the way she went with it—that was all she ever lived for.

D R E S S

"She would go to the beach alone"

Once as she came flying along the beach on her bare feet, the big picture hat[1] sliding back and forth from scapula to scapula, she stubbed one of her toes on a brick[2] that had certainly, she yelped, hopping about on the other, uninjured foot, not been there the day before when a confusion of currents coming from several directions at once and yet all the while, beneath the surface, not fooling around in the least, but moving *away* from the shore, had nearly dragged her out to sea.

[1] "The better to see THE BIG PICTURE," she had explained to the milliner who was measuring her head, suggesting a light but durable material, proposing a flattering shape, and a tie so that when she did break into a run crossing the dunes, the hat could jostle around happily over the flaxen hair raveling down to her waist.

[2] The brick was one of the inert members of the corps de ballet in *The Toes of Nichevo*, the narration in both ballet and radio play accompanied by a band of people brushing their teeth loaned out for the occasions by the producer of *The Telltale Toothbrush*, enjoying a snappy run at a small theater in the West End:

"In the next cottage lived a brick-layer and a woman and another woman," (the narrator continued). "Not what you'd call kept women themselves, they kept his house and kept each other smiling, for he went far to lay his bricks and they often went for weeks with neither hide nor hair of him. So by now he had laid one brick. He tore it out and took it to the beach. There were nine more left to get laid . . ."

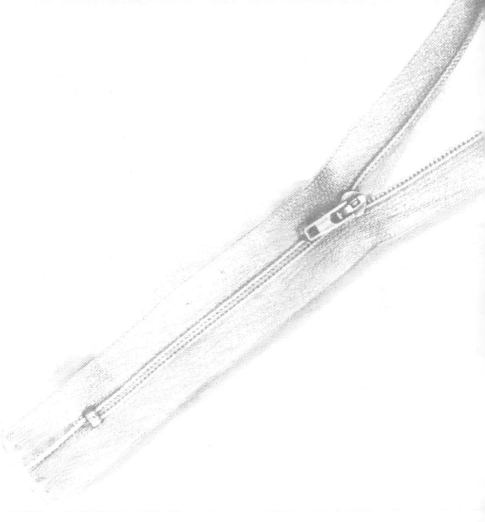

Espadrilles

(from *The Red Shoes*)

Why couldn't she breeze into a room and kick off her espadrilles like other girls? Would she never be able to wash her socks at the village fountain in the morning while the housefronts were being scrubbed, or see her own translucent toenails like seashells in the sun? What must it feel like to slide her soles along fresh white sheets, or to twitch her toes beneath the covers in the afterglow of love?

Flounces

(from *The Red Shoes*)

She had been a fractious child, but as she grew out of the toy tea sets and flounces of littlegirlhood, and her honey-colored hair deepened into a thicker, even richer luster, a sweetness oozed into her nature and stuck to her every act and gesture toward the brutes and the frail alike.

Frock

(from *The Red Shoes*)

She would have loved to drape her stockings over a wild rosebush, wriggle out of her dirndl,* and plunge into the swirling waters of a stream, or enjoy the embrace of a passing wayfarer like any young girl with a soft down on her upper lip and a generous current of her own streaming through her eager limbs, but always they were there, the weight, the clumsiness, even in the ravishment, the heels clacking together around the waist of her partner as her legs climbed the air and her voice rose to the heights her pleasure had reached, just a moment before.

* Yes, dirndls are Austrian frocks, but this girl's great-aunt Elsbeth had come home from a ski trip in the Tyrol,* and brought back, half out of pity for the child since she could not get those things strapped into skis, and if she could, one hates to contemplate the jeopardy of their dancing over the icy slopes as they pleased, and half out of the usual great-auntness that prompts the bearing of such gifts, a pink-and-white dirndl with silver buttons and bright blue trim, which she wore in the summertime although it clashed rather sadly with the scarlet shoes.

* Aunt Elsbeth had gone with a Croatian seamstress named Anja with whom she had corresponded for five years before their meeting by sending scraps of their work to each other and inspecting each other's stitchery, exchanging notes on the

various problems each one faced in achieving the flawless buttonhole, collar, or hem. Elsbeth had spent hours trying to imagine the size, texture of Anja's hands, the length and condition of her fingernails, while Anja wondered if she, Elsbeth, laid her work in her lap mostly, or held it closer to her face, in case she were slightly myopic, or to give herself better light as it streamed in over her left shoulder. These were not matters for their correspondence, however, as if at some point this tacit agreement had been reached, and so their musings began with and returned to the material world they shared. The two aging women walked about Innsbruck with their arms around one another's waists, rode narrow-gage railroads through white alpine tunnels, and flirted with all sorts of men. By day they flew down the slopes in their heavy woolen coats, and by night they rocked the rafters of a succession of dark-timbered lodges with laughter they had saved up for years, for just such an outburst at last as this one, and they parted after three weeks of such behavior like the friskiest of girlhood friends with a lifetime of crooked seams ahead.

F R O C K

Long before Cinderella, her skirt floating about her like fallen wings,[1] glided down the stairs from the powder room to equivocate around the dance floor with the prince and loll in a corner behind a potted palm catching their runaway breaths,[2] the two seamstresses had cut out her wedding dress, matched it with Valenciennes lace, and were carrying on a long-distance collaboration over pieces of it, in addition to the work for their regular customers, Elsbeth trying to keep her afflicted niece in becoming attire, Anja's cruises, etc. But when she came to that scene with the orchids and meringue, Elsbeth sent a postcard to Anja in the Dutch West Indies saying, "Hold off on the bodice a while yet. I have this feeling she may not be going through with it. I've just done up a jacket of fustian[3] for a morose and ugly man," to which Anja replied, with her habitual cryptic brevity, "Syntax the Tailor, my dear"—unless it was a message garbled by the ship's purser in a telegram sent at sea.

1   "Why should wings stick out only from shoulder blades?" she wrote in her diary later that night, remembering how light she had felt.

2   "I told him lots of likely stories and waited for my heart to leap into his mouth."

3   I *did* come across a review the other day (in same magazine with Jacob Other's piece on a poem "New York Boogie-Woogie" that lays down the rules of a game to play in the painting by Mondrian) of the pallid author's pastoral prose. "Slung together with bits of fustian" is one phrase that leaps to mind.

Furbelows

How he wished to get past her furbelows, to shorten her distant gazes, and fill her long pauses with the lowings of a thousand wanton cows.

As he herded her into his notion of who he thought she was, the cows ambled aimlessly over his piece of hot property and beyond the bounds of his beliefs.

Gloves

(from _Life in the Forest Sauvage_)

She sank her slight buttocks onto the bench
with gusto and wiggled into her new kid gloves.

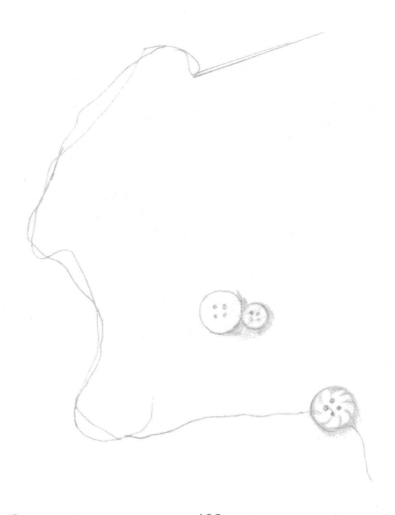

Hairshirt

(from *Life in the Forest Sauvage*)

He dropped his hairshirt off with his
coiffeur for a shampoo, cream rinse,
and trim.

Hat

DEATH IN VENICE HAT

She bought a black velvet hat and chased a
little boy in a sailor suit all over town.
When she wanted to sleep the *signor* would
then appear and row her straight out to sea,
a tropical disease.

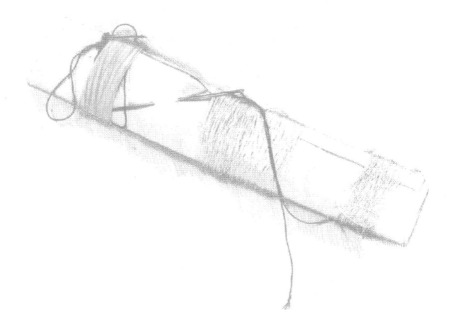

Kimono

Morpheus, the nights are breaking over me, like your body demanding mine, but it goes on, this voice of a voracious woman, whether or not you're here to listen, to yell, "Stop thrashing around!" while holding me down or, "Stop bleating!" as the wool catches on fences between me and sleep and I collect it to make blankets for all the women and children of the world twitching with fears and desire. It always feels like I'm trying on your love, so no wonder you sent me the kimono, like slinking into something, and sometimes I can't tell if I'm putting it on or taking it off, the way it is with any truly agreeable garment, somehow better than nothing at all: how you enwrapture me! These thicknesses passing over and pressing through me, the denseness and lightness floating and sinking, and us: a stranger I keep becoming a part of, unsure of how much of myself to pour into it, how much of you to mix with, assuring myself that I can get through anything alone, even get through being with you. But of course I will never get away with that, and you got away with me this morning before I could hold on to a last sensation of you, a promise you'll be there again.

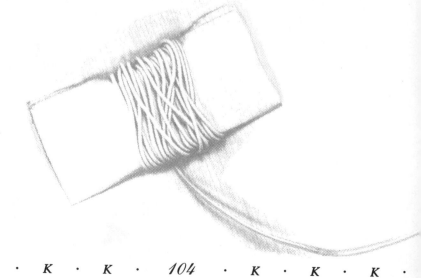

Lava-Lava

(from *The Little Match Girl*)

Teeth of winter, sinking into my flesh, my own clacking against each other like knitting needles, and I wish they'd knit a heavy shawl around my shoulders before widening into a yawn. Why do I always yawn when I'm cold? I think of the star that's a frozen toe tossed into the sky by Thor. If only . . . the only teeth that are clacking are the ones slung with shells around my neck and tossing to and fro, biting at the torpid sunbeams of a Gauguin afternoon, luscious, frothy, I could eat that sky with a spoon. Like one of those tropical cocktails that have such vulgar names, juices of mango, guava, passion fruit dribble down my chin, plashing onto my belly as I undulate in my lava-lava with a flamingo on a leash. My tangled hair, streaked with salt and sunlight, damp with sweat, semen, fructose, is plastered to my shoulder blades and clings to my bouncing breasts, my navel crusty with submarine minerals from a recent plunge in the sea. Among our legs, the flamingo's and mine, entwine our lovers of various sexes and species, with iridescent insects crawling across their overlapping furs, feathers, and skins, a drum in the distance setting up its beat in my heart. The flamingo molting in our mingled footprints, I am drenched, brimming, my fur hands, stripped and pink, coaxing one of the nearby bodies into a state of arousal while I sink onto my knees and sear his senses with the flames licking out of my fingertips as I light another match and cup its warmth to my face.

Nightgown

He was awakened at the creak of dawn by a flannel flapping sound. Although it had no knees to speak of, a long-
sleeved nightgown with rows of roses climbing blue-and-
white lattices knelt in the doorway waving its lace-cuffed
arms and swaying from side to side to a rhythm he
couldn't quite put his finger on, but which smacked of
Africa.

As he soon discovered, the flannel nightgown was
in fact a gospel singer, and regaled him with its sabbath
repertoire until the first rays of daylight broke in on the
shadows of that full-bodied voice, which disappeared
into a laundry chute. This gave his silk dressing gown
something to think about after he'd slammed the door
on his breakfast of solitude and caught the tramway of
travail. What sweet emotions those folds of flannel had
evoked! No matter that the hands that might have been
clapping were now rubbing the contralto over the wash-
board as its mouth filled up with soap and the Hallelujahs
caused large bubbles to burst in the sun. The silk dressing gown, which had never been immersed in such stuff
in its life, nor submitted to an abrasive touch on its fine
and many-colored threads, made sure the coast was clear
before stepping into the hallway and entering a new life
before the mirror of gyrations and fervor theretofore in
its murkiest dreams unspun.

NIGHTGOWN

Another instance of the sort of thing not to be missed in
doorways, as a glance through any DOOR should show.

"disappeared into a laundry chute"
This can't be the same laundry room we encountered in the
note to that last and watchful TIME, Timofey's *remorse*—a
netherworld where the nightgown, belching Allelujahs,
would appear an unseemly guest. Although, come to think
of it, that couple stripping beside the basement washers and
dryers in UNDERSHIRT . . .

Pajamas

Bon giorno!

Your letter tracked me down at the American Express in Rome, a city they seem to be giving back to the wolves (well, I was propositioned only three times today between my morning capuccino and lunch, over which I am dawdling, the polenta with octopus all inky like this note, and far from home, like me). Rumors reaching me that my last book was said to have been written by "a chic lesbian living in Rome," I decided I'd avoided this part of Italy too long, and swerved down here through Orvieto and a night on a floor above a hillside village bakery because a baby had arrived to occupy the guest room I'd been offered two years before. I see you are learning to make ideas take off their pajamas, and that's one way of getting at the naked truth. I've been undressing the authors who hide in me, but so far have unearthed no Albert Camus. Here comes *il addizione*. And an espressoed kiss.

Yolanta

Pants

Still in the Marais, whose streets are as dark and closed as this December. I notice that in German, my multilingual corduroy pants, made in Scotland but thrown out at me by someone in London before they got to the jumble sale, are made of *baumwolle*—tree wool. Upstairs in the hotel, the Panamaniac's library is being built, and all his books, transported from Spain, are covered with fluffs of dust called *moutons*—sheep (did they pick these up crossing the Pyrenees?) Books being made of trees, sheep coming to rest on books, forests sprouting fleece, I conclude that my lower garments deserve further study. My hands read the lines in corduroy curving over my thighs, and a mutual understanding is reached.

"read the lines in corduroy"
See the Yolanta note to FACE where she's perusing a story-lined cheek.

Pelisse

As the pelisse slid from her generous shoulders and tumbled onto the tumulus of wraps on the bed—cloaks, fur coats, capes (she noticed a red one a bit shredded around the hood)—she caught sight of a small figure flickering at the window through the frosted pane, and her hand reached to rearrange the warm jewels at her throat, just like St. Agnes' Eve, she thought, wondering of whom she would dream in the coming dawn, and at the rough little beast outside.

P E L I S S E

"rough little beast"
Obviously the little match girl at the window, growing shaggier by the minute in her tango with the wolf, her teeth tearing at her own flesh, the fur hands sharpening their nails. But the pelisse itself was a *modèle* called "Slouching Toward Bethlehem," as the label sewn to its furry lining read.

Petticoats

(from The Glass Shoe)

In the year 186–, Miss A– was just beginning to become aware of a number of new, though not entirely unpleasant, sensations in the region enlaced by her petticoats, somewhere between her navel and her knees . . .

"Miss A—"
A pale outline of a figure in *Loose Women and Tight Corners.**
Cinders dusted her cheeks with ashes and Nature Morte
Blusher to suffuse them with the quiet commotion the es-
capades on the ensuing pages richly rewarded and amplified.

* The enormous success this coloring book had—in such far-flung
places as Constantinople, where it scored as big a hit with the
eunuchs as with their fluttering charges, and a clinic in Switzerland,
whose director found therapeutic applications for its games among
his malaised matrons—led to a sequel called *Loose Women in Tight
Clothing,* with a mail-order catalogue of garb attached, and under-
sizing advice offered for its wet T-shirts and constricting nighties
to crawl out of the minute chance came crashing through the shrub-
bery and bashing down one's door.*

> * The last bit of this sentence was stolen from *Sleepless Beauty,*
> about a loquacious insomniac, as were the so-called "Sonnets
> to Morpheus," mere previews of the *accouchements* to come.

Pockets

Whenever she cooked dinner, she kept
her apron pockets stuffed with caramels
made of little sayings of Emily Dickinson.

Stuffing her skirt into its own
pockets, she looked for something
to hide.

She pocketed the change
hoping everything would
remain the same.

No, I won't live in your pocket.
It's too dark down there, and
I'd always be slapping your thigh.

He told me to keep in touch
so I chopped off his finger
to carry in my pocket.

She worked her way into his
pocket, looking for a short
cut to take him by surprise.

There was once a little girl
who had a little pocket
right in the middle of her
thighs.

P O C K E T S

"once a little girl"
Mistakenly identified by Jacob Other as a nursery rhyme from
Guillaume des Forêts' *Trois oies dans une babushka*, this is
actually a translation back into English of a chapter in *La Vie
in the Wild Forest* by Danielle Mémoire, whose admirable *Le
Biscuit inachevé* is on its way out of the ovens at Pantagruel
Press.

Pockets

**She broke out in a case of small
pockets and a cholera of fur.**

P O C K E T S

"a cholera of fur"

When she slunk her nappy eminence into the Schwarzwald
doctor's praxis for a third visit, he carefully avoided encour-
aging false expectations of ever shedding this strange growth
she had found rather cozy through the first blustery winter,
but an encumbrance and embarrassment at Bayreuth the following July. "You're just banging your fur head against the
wall,"[1] he told the girl straight out with kindness but no
mercy, stroking a shaggy forearm and making a mental note
to put something in her file about the healthy sheen this pelt
had recently acquired.

The small pockets also brought a swarm of new troubles,
a motley procession of beggars trailing after her wherever
she went. On an Istrian holiday, and exasperated by the local
mendicants' attentions, she whipped out a phrase book and
let them have it in Serbo-Croatian,[2] word spread, and they
let her stray about unmauled for the remaining days she had
in Rovinj.

[1] See WALL.
[2] *"Varate se asko mislite da su mi džepovi puni novčanica."* "If you
think my pockets are lined with banknotes, you are mistaken."

Pockets

**The future ran past
with a hole in its pocket
and gold standards nailed
to its knees.**

POCKETS

"and gold standards nailed to its knees"

It eventually met up with the hypochondriac at a clinic in Switzerland. They both beat it as fast as they could, faking speedy recoveries. The place was crawling with middle-aged matrons and blushing young grandmothers all suffering from a peculiar set of symptoms becoming more virulent long after marriage and childbirth but apparently related to their having had too many gold stars plastered to their foreheads when young. This, anyway, was the only thing the puzzled doctors could determine these patients had in common aside from the usual things such a collection of women might share.

Pockets

**I live in a pocket of misery
lined with shredded silk.**

POCKETS

"a pocket of misery"

Yolanta, of her hovel in the Marais or life in general, come to collect 200 francs for "La Mode et la muse" from the editor of *Passion*.

Pockets

**200 francs for
two small tickets!
Two small tickets
tripping down the
street like
skeletons with pockets.**

"200 francs for two small tickets!"
From a bilingual dream Yolanta's first night in London after a channel crossing by Hovercraft. The second, French half went:

> *Comme être approchée d'un avenir*
> *qui est un squelette avec des poches.*
> Like being approached by a future
> that's a skeleton with pockets.

Pockets play a poignant part in the final scene of *The Little Match Girl*, too. When they find her frozen body the following morning, they discover a note in her coat pocket reminding her to mend her pocket.

Pockets

(from *The Gingerbread Variations*)

> **For my dead brother**
> **has no hands**
> **to put in them.**

"dead brother"
Gretl, again assuming the worst. Actually, his hands were quite busy working over the witch's trapezius and quadratus before the nightly frolics began.

Purse

An old lady gets on the bus and rubs her commodious white leather purse against my arm. It feels pleasant, but I give her a dirty look just to let her know I know that I've been aggressed by a dead cow carrying her eyedrops and handkerchief.

P U R S E

From Yolanta's little book *Carnet*, of bus and métro rides the ten yellow tickets took her on. Hence the Erotic Transport of BRA. The book was a beautiful handmade object sold to collectors, and published and painted by Passera in Caen.

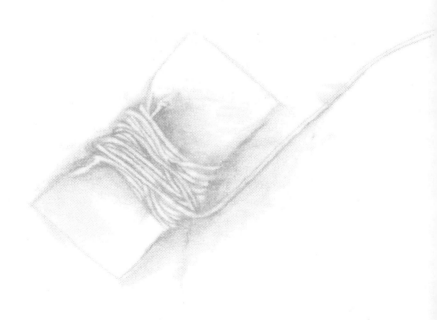

Ring

(from *The Shattered Glass Slipper: Reflections in a Broken Shoe*)*

I pulled on my rings and blue stockings and spent the rest of the afternoon clanking about in my costume jewelry, knocking them off their feet with bons mots and aperçus, clinking my high heels together, and wishing I hadn't come.

* A subvariant of *The Glass Shoe.*

Scarf

And then came winter, with her raw hands, her blue lips, her angora scarf lashed raffishly about her scraggy neck.

S C A R F

"And then came winter"

One reason for these cruises of Anja's was to escape the influenzas that visited her country* this time each year, and things were no better in Paris, see FUR, or Morocco, and God knows what she might pick up from some sad case in a Swiss sanitorium, so she took to the placid seas with their languid, shufflebored passengers and the phosphorescences dancing upon waves an evening stroll on deck might reveal, at the sign of the first snowstorm, or chill of the first blasting wind.

* In *Life in the Forest Sauvage*, "a plague of Reason broke out and was ravaging the country, snatching little girls right out of their pinafores and mudpies, and shoving them into bookkeeping classes before they could even brush their bangs off their furrowed little foreheads or finish the arabesques of candy hearts and raisins upon which they had been so intent."

Scarves

In their white scarves, dark glasses, and dirty Cadillac, they sat idling on the lowest level of the parking structure (she reading a map, he keeping his eye on the windshield and a firm grip on the wheel) until the last traces of gasoline had been exhausted and the scenery dissolved.

Schmatte

(from *The Glass Shoe*)

I scratched my schmatte and
proceeded with the floor.

S C H M A T T E

Cinderella, or Cendrine, as she is called in "Cendrine and
the Garçon Flambé," a video by Jean-Jacques Passera, picked
up a few Yiddish expressions from the shops in the village,
so it is not surprising to come across entries in her diary like:
"I was polishing the tsatskelehs when the doorbell rang and
I opened the door to a dwarf selling hairbrushes" or "I
schlepped my bucket up the front stairs to do Agfa's room,
but her door was locked and a sign that read MUSE PLEASE
dangled from the doorknob, so I figured she was at it with
her pathetic fallacies, and tiptoed off for *une petite somme* in
the attic instead."

Shirt

Dear Morpheus,
    I said it silently, many times last night, which turned
into morning somewhere in the shirt and smooth skin
you slipped into, somewhere in the folds you opened in
the darkness so weightless that I felt you, next to me,
and earlier across the room, as someone who really hadn't
been there before.

Love,
K

$\mathcal{S}hoes$

(from *The Red Shoes*)

Actually, she quite liked these nights spent at the cobbler's, and it was even whispered in the village that she deliberately scraped them knocking into things and wore them out faster than such knocking about could account for just so she could fall asleep exhausted in the cobbler's arms with the smell of shoe polish filling her quiet breathing and shining the footgear of her dreams, her lips parted and her right fist jammed against her cheekbone* as the clocks sounded in the *horlogerie* next door.

* Her fine cheekbones were already emerging as a strength in her features, the way they lifted her face out toward the temples and cradled her dark eyes. This is something that does not always show in a girl during those years when her flesh seems to be rearranging itself every other day, modeling itself to the skeletal structure and the shape of womanhood trying to find the form, and settle into it, that this particular female will inhabit for the rest of her life—now grabbing with handfuls at her hipbones, now swelling out her calves, suddenly snapping her into a pliant sapling, crushing her into tiers of anguished tissues, then rolling her up in a mattress* and sending her off to her husband's house. But Red Shoes had a precocious face.

> * The mattress at the cobbler's was made for one large person, which he certainly was, but her young and supple body made room for itself as she slipped into his embrace and sought his caresses, her cries holding onto him melting through the clocks on the other side of the yes and she was reaching the other   her hair slapped across his face   the air   and chest   jerked back over her shudders before she crashed onto his ample surface and lay twitching in the laughter rising out of her hunger that hovered over the room of shoes all laced up and nowhere to walk through her sudden stillness for once and at last and again

Skirt

(from *The Little Match Girl*)

It was not always matches I had to offer to whoever was happening by my outstretched hand. After the holidays it was tulips—yellow, red, and cream. The rich tones of these cream tulips especially pleased me and drew me into them, down to the drop at the center where all thickness and warmth seemed to rest and begin. These flowers, at once goblets and bright or pale flames, do not really have faces or skirts. They are interiors folded back and falling into themselves. I don't care about the sexual significance of all this, and the comparisons men have made between my opening to their mouths and the trembling of rose petals at dawn as the beast of day comes to drink from them. I am rather inaccessible as a woman, being more like a cross between a small girl and a man, which is confusing to others to discover in my hesitant and possessing embrace—while mistaking me for the very embodiment of how they have always wished to be desired. It is true that there is this want dragging around in me, and that no one can help but attempt to feed it, and because I am sweet and this state of pleasure in abeyance pours off me almost continually though I am ill at ease and shabbily clothed, everyone finds himself entering with pleasure also into this hunger and allowing himself to be completely devoured.

Sleeves

Pressed between two sleeves rubbing their tweeds against her bare upper arms, and two voices with them that scratched several exposed sensibilities around the table and rasped at each other across her face, she wafted her way out of the commingling bouquets of champagne and several resinous reds (or was it a touch of licorice teased out of an oaken cask?) and hurled herself into a passing dumbwaiter headed for what levels of meaning awaited her in the lower depths.

S L E E V E S

One of those celebrated birthday dinners at Chez Panisse. Though in fact she was already as low as she could go and there wasn't a dumbwaiter in sight.

Slip

His gnarled hand held onto her raincoat long after she'd given him the slip.

S L I P

I hope this isn't the peasant's daughter in TUTU. If it is, though, it can't be her father's hand, as he was still young and fit, so her molester would have been some old tramp who appeared at the pantry door looking for a few days' work or a mug of kvass. If it *was* kvass, made from rye crumbs, then this tale is closer to BABUSHKA than it seems, for the blini woman was always using crumbs* every which way in her viatic feasts. And then, Hansel and Gretl fled the jaws of death inside the gingerbread by following the crumbs of *The Unfinished Cookie* through the forest—a cycle recounting the reassuring gestures and silent reproaches of mothers from ancient to present times. ("Her thumbprint in the oatmeal cookie!" "I know she sees me with the eyes in the back of her headache." "The implacable inside mother, who won't graciously abandon me!" "He came to an island covered with mothers," etc.) If it *was* the budding ballerina who answered the door, she was wearing her raincoat because either the roof was leaking on a rainy day or she had been pirouetting about in her makeshift tutu and flung on the first garment her own hand fell upon in a dark closet modesty compelled her to open at the sound of the bum's rap.

* "It's nothing but crumbs!" I cried late one night when a friend showed up to distract me from my typewriter. *"Oui, mais on peut faire un très bon gâteau des miettes."**

> * "Yes, but you can make a very good cake* out of crumbs." The French should be read with a Yugoslavian accent, not quite Serbian, not quite Slovenian.

>> * "These notes keep unfolding in my lap, as my life moves from café to *métro* stop to stairway, and it's all getting folded into the cake batter, to be poured into those rattled cake pans* you already know about."
>>   —from a letter then

>   * See JAR.

Socks

**Red socks beneath black piano,
play me some blue notes, baby.**

S   O   C   K   S

"Red socks"
The *enfant terrible* of WATCH listening to Jeremy Menuhin at Châtelet, and very much taken with the bit of resplendent ankle lighting up the stage.

In the wedding vows Cinderella is composing to exchange with her prince, in lawful deadlock, his initial assent comes in response to: "Would you trust this woman with your socks?"

Socks

(from *Don Juan Is a Woman*)

Don Juan is a woman because she's so curious, and she's hotter than any room she walks into, though she can't tell the difference, the way she feels the outside brushing against grabbing stroking scratching spitting on her coming in under her dress up around her knees and slowly circling them. The world is a current jolting through her, a breath opening her many mouths and pulling apart her every seamless gesture in any direction   away from her   into her   tossing her softly off her tiptoes affronting the feigned freight in her eyes   slipping her so gently out of her italics, her stammering parentheses, her gloves of lace and socks of twine. So much to go around, so many laps to land in, so many beaux jesters rocking her hoarse cries into the scarlet corners gathering at the center of the room   shaping her sleep in the *couvertures*.

S   O   C   K   S

"hotter than any room"
See also FEVER.

"feigned freight in her eyes"
Since it *was* she of whom was said "she's a bright, sudden train wreck on an uneventful day," perhaps a freight train was chugging across her frontal bone, headed for a collision with his train of thought.

"her stammering parentheses"
Yolanta had to give quite some thought to this before deciding that it didn't really belong in her anthology of things going on between parentheses in women's literature of all time. It was roughly at *this* time that Jacob Other, letting himself into her studio on rue de Birague (she had moved from that *pénible chambre de bonne* up seven flights of stairs),

discovered her, licking the *confiture de framboises* (see grandmotherly note to red BOOTS) off her fingers, with a bookmark between her legs.

"socks of twine"
Still, she did give the work a footnote in a piece she wrote for *Passion* called "La Mode et la muse": "In *Don Juan Is a Woman*, she is wearing gloves of lace and socks of twine. *Twine* twists into *entwine*, and other ways of disporting about a lover's body, or how a bougainvillea can carry on with a drainpipe."

"hoarse cries into the scarlet corners"
See the crescendo of SHOES.

"shaping her sleep in the couvertures*"*
See the unravaged solitude of MOOD.

Stockings

Not only was her memory as sheer as her stockings, but each thing it held shone through every other one so vividly that all were hopelessly suffused. A street in midtown Manhattan ran through a pitcher of Löwenbrau she'd once shared with Dragomir Mirković on the banks of the Rhine so that one of its street lamps lit up the foam as it touched his lips, and a look he had given her later yet that evening stabbed the hard heart she had turned on him two years afterward in Salzburg in such a way that the blood poured into her empty glass on that same table as he offered her another round of beer and imagined the child she would bear him if all went according to his plans.

Stockings

Loneliness: An emaciated woman who stands on the sidewalk with a furled umbrella saying to everyone who walks past her, "I'm awfully sorry to have to be saying good-bye to you." She looks like Mad Meg in Breughel's painting with her hair pulled back, wears pale grey stockings, and has big feet. She's standing on them. And who wouldn't? It's going to rain.

S T O C K I N G S

The mermaids may not have had legs, but every now and then on a slow afternoon they liked to sprawl on the rocks pretending they did, swapping isometric exercises to keep their thighs firm and shapely, complaining about their cellulite or varicose veins, and saying things to one another* about the day's catch like, "And what did your fishnet stockings drag down this time?"

* Their phosphorescent chatter was not limited to fantasy appendages and garments they'd never seen. The mermaids reveled in a very rich oral tradition drawn from the flora and fauna of their aqueous underworld, so one of them might say, halfway through an anecdote about a tiff with some pal: ". . . and then her eyes turned the color of barking seals, and she stormed off into a bed of kelp to sulk and call me names I won't repeat."

Sweater

Today I went to the Museum of Costume and Fashion to read Diderot through clothes—"La Littérature et la mode." The place was full of old ladies knitting sweaters on benches and gabbling in the foyer while Emily Bovary's wedding was being enacted in a dim niche within. I should have helped myself to one off the clicking needles! I need some more layers of wool to bundle me through the rest of this winter, and cannot stand the

"Vous désirez?" that greets me in every shop, turning so swiftly, after the *"Ah, c'est une merveille, c'est tout à fait pour vous, Madame"* or *"Que c'est chouette!"* from the younger set, to the chilliest scene, the coldest shoulder if my interest in the mirror flickers—and the thin lips press together into a slit of avaricious malice as the sweater is coolly taken from my hands.

S W E A T E R

One of the postcards home to her jar, confidante and guardian of some of Yolanta's best-kept secrets, from the weeks of research for "La Mode et la muse." Several years later she raided the jar and several friends' drawers to reconstruct her mapped and tattered winters of hovels and esplanades.

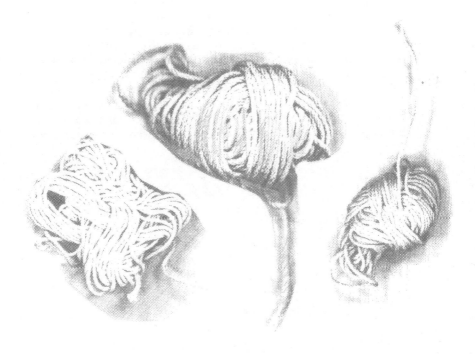

T-Shirt

(from *The Red Shoes*)

Elsbeth never gave a thought to bringing out a line of Hans Christian Andersen T-shirts, even though she knew someone who knew someone who knew him, and through this chain of acquaintances, found herself making him the jacket* he wore on his rambles through Italy with an uncle or grandfather of Karen Blixen; and he'd pounced on the story of her niece's shoes and twisted it into a depressing, moralizing Protestant sermon while the child herself was off on the road to the Balkans giving an eyeful to a tavern of merchants all Eastward bound with their flasks of schnapps, or brandy made of whatever Mother Nature had deposited on their summer hillsides, and the goods they would be unloading in exchange for silks and spices somewhere in the Orient.

* Yolanta, whose literary delusions were wrapping more and more cozily about her own person, started dressing up in dust jackets when the nip of autumn arrived in Paris, and it was thus she was attired the morning the *boulanger* darted a disbelieving glance at her feet in BREAD and wondered if The Girl Who Trod on the Loaf had come to Paris, too, recalling that the Andersen tale begins "and of how she came to a bad end," for he was having a bout of homesickness for his native Dordogne, and the City of Light seemed a dubious fate for him and his wife and this nice girl of Polish descent.

T-Shirt

T-SHIRTS OF BYZANTIUM

To W. B. Yeats:

This is no country for old men.
It's a place where little gold
parking lots are kept.

The one to W. B. Yeats, who, during his Crazy Jane period, liked to romp about in the high winds on moonless nights wearing his MAUD'S GONE T-shirt and wishing the circus animals, too, would come back to his empyrean tent. This T-shirt's earlier title (now "Driving through Byzantium"), before the grimy veneer was removed from its gilded surface, was "Céline to Byzantium." About the narrative I've been haranguing you with, Céline might well have added to whatever else you're thinking: "She was waxing devilish eloquent. The hope of extricating herself from this shady mess at last was making the old bitch* lyrical after her own filthy fashion."

* See note to TABLE, the one at the seaside café, not the one with Beaujolais stains on a white tablecloth and dessert spoons waving in a circle* of gesticulating hands.

> * Don't see CIRCLE. At the most one of them would have thought to bring along a stash of toffee in his pocket to see him through the interminable sessions of soul-baring he attended only because the cook was quite good. They soon stopped inviting him, anyway, when his comments diminished to a laconic "UMM. UMM."—a favorite line of his from a Mishima play, but not the sort of empathy one was expected to exude at these things.

T-Shirt

(from *Colored Clothes for Covered Moments*)

BLUE T-SHIRT

> Blue is a house that requires no key.
> It is not locked, it is not looked for.
> You can stumble into it any time, slowly
> or suddenly, and come up floating on your
> back. It is kind, and sorry, and you are
> alone in it.

"kind, and sorry"

A forgivable misunderstanding of Ezra Pound's *Condensare*. But I don't know if he ever forgave her:

> Greta garbled.
> Ezra pounded her.

T-Shirt

(from *Elemental T-Shirts*)

WET T-SHIRT

> Well, I just felt like putting on something to wear and I feel safe in it. Elbows like wings. Waters of endless reflection. A covering that ripples when you, wind, shiver me to wetness.

"Wet T-Shirt"

All Jacob Other had to say about this vapid little poem of Jonquil's was: "As your thoughts improve, your ideas dissolve." Another one in this elemental series, "The Auberge of the Flying Hearth," combines two elements in Montgolfier's discovery of the hot air balloon while drying his wife's chemise over the fireplace.

Tutu

(from *The Red Shoes*)

The cobbler's shop, a mere shoebox clamped between the tailor's and the *horlogerie*, had wooden feet that squatted in the window like stunned ducks; devices that squeezed and whirred; little drawers full of nails that looked old and shiny; unattached heels that knew nothing yet of aimless wandering; and shelves from floor to ceiling with pairs* of boots and shoes waiting to be reclaimed.

* The cobbler did not like it if someone brought in one shoe all by itself. Sometimes a peasant would walk for miles with one disorganized boot in his hand, the one not holding his wayfarer's lunch of sheep's milk cheese from Corsica wrapped in pimientos and *herbes de Provence*, a good crusty bread, with a sole worn through or coming unstitched and pulling away from the rest of the foot; or a toe cracked from sloshing and standing in mud, in soil cooking with fresh manure—and this peasant, after a pleasant repast on this day off from his own land and responsibilities and the weary, accusing regard of his wife and the smudged faces of his children who worked willingly enough but with faraway looks in their eyes.*

* Where his daughter got the idea of being a ballet dancer is beyond the scope of this story's speculations, but it was heartrending to see her in the mock tutu she had fashioned out of an old mail-order catalogue slip of pale pink with white laces crossing from the waist up to her clavicles. She had installed a dance studio in a corner of the barn from pieces of mirror found lying broken on a heap of stained glass crates from Belgium behind the glazier's. Along one wall ran a bar she clutched* at as one foot held the ground and the other rose and fell through arcs cut over the dusty surface of the floor.

* He would arrrive, by this time clutching the boot in the other hand, after a half day of reveries and extensive vistas over the flat countryside and some irritating thoughts this changing landscape could not mollify or vanquish, and the cobbler would greet him cordially but with discouragement, for he could not accept one shoe alone.*

And so the peasant was obliged to trudge back to his farm with its fence sliding into fallible angles, the trouble with the weather, the vicissitudes of all these shoots forever pushing out of the ground, of all these pigs, cows, geese never ceasing to dance for his attention, and the damp and impatient budding beauty of his youngest child, whose good-night kisses had been recently too demanding, too prolonged.

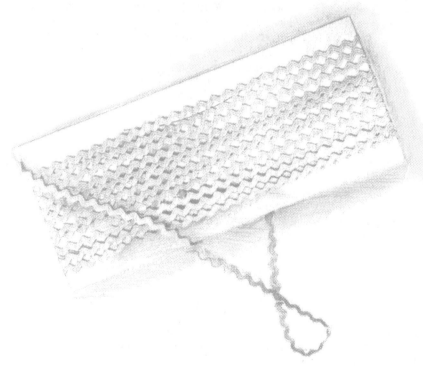

Umbrella

Why do I have the impression that I am clutching an umbrella as I fall asleep?

In my dream I am visiting a cemetery. At the entrance to this necropolis is a library full of books on the many ways to die. But they are, of course, the ones we've been reading, and the ones we are about to begin.

U M B R E L L A

"a library full of books"
Yolanta's dream, exquisite corpse.

Undershirt

You come blundering through my dreams with your undershirt on upside down and your Tierra del Fuego cologne.

U N D E R S H I R T

"your Tierra del Fuego cologne"
Torquil did go off to Patagonia "to try and forget" soon after Jonquil had dumped him on his own doorstep and abandoned herself to that other tempestuous affair.

Undershirt

Home from another Sunday drive in the parking structure, with their exhausted clothing tumbling among lost socks and soap, they sat in the laundromat playing strip poker, she starting with the charms of her bracelet, he moving on to his undershirt, after, of course, his curlers,

and the pink hairnet flashing with sequins that matched
his chamazulene eyes.

U N D E R S H I R T

"their exhausted clothing"
See SCARVES.

"lost socks and soap"
This would intimate things lost on you and me to the muslin
dummy in SCAR.

"playing strip poker"
The game continues in *Frangipani's Pajamas*, but the stakes
and players are changed, and it's set in a seraglio.

"flashing with sequins"
In Bedruthan's story of COMB, a mermaid is sewing sequins
onto her tail. Or am I sewing sequences onto my tale? I just
exhumed one fluttering little scrap from the pale author, too:
"Ask not for whom the tale is told. It's told by me."

"chamazulene eyes"
The only reason his eyes are so identified is the shampoo
made from this rare flower so recently rinsed from his lustrous hair, the luster, I suppose, owing to the African Butter
Herb in the formula. The one time Anja had given Morocco
a whirl, she drank a tea of Moroccan blue camomile to calm
a queasy stomach—a lovely blue liquid glistening in an icy
glass on a terrace with too much sun.

Wedding Train

To the end of her days she dragged her wedding train around with her and lived happily ever after him.

He unfolded her for the rest of his life.

WEDDING TRAIN

"He unfolded her for the rest of his life"

In the not so intimate parallel play of another marriage, the peasant tried to *unravel* his wife (see note to DRESS), but by the end of the day he had little stamina for such tussles, what with getting up long before sunrise to stagger about in a state of beatitude listening to the lowing of his wanton cows, and then roaming over his property for hours admiring God's nimble handiwork in every pistil, stamen, and seed, and so he abandoned himself at bedtime to his flannel pajamas, eating pistachios, and reading escapist metafictions like *A Doll Among the Jungle*, by Jean-Jacques Passera: "Losing the thread of her story in the jungle, she removed the heroine's pith helmet and ran her smudged fingers distractedly through the typewriter ribbon tangled in the runaway debutante's matted hair."

Zipper

The afternoon sun slid along her buttocks like a lost zipper.

(Note to artist: Well, actually, I picture a Sisyphus who seems to have forgotten what he is supposed to be doing, going uphill with considerable difficulty and a rough stone, and instead is gliding the sun, its glorious golden sphere, along a beautiful body lying nice and flat and naked and curvaceously on the feverish grass.)

Z I P P E R

"uphill with considerable difficulty"
Although the lay of the land is similar, this isn't the guy being tormented in Yolanta's *The Mistress of Sisyphus*. And what a tease *she* is, treating her lover to the same unending struggle Camus likens to our own.

"a beautiful body lying nice and flat"
The body of this book, intimately unappareled.

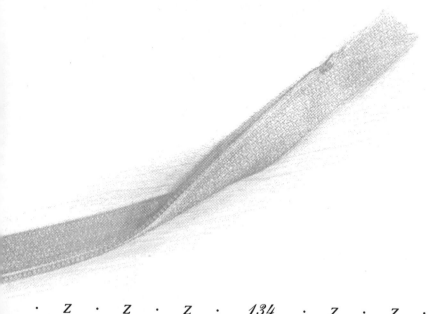

ABOUT THE AUTHOR

Karen Elizabeth Gordon is the author of *The Well-Tempered Sentence* and *The Transitive Vampire*. She lives in northern California and keeps closets in the Tyrol and France.